Preface

Microsoft Azure Virtual Desktop AZ 140: Microsoft Azure Virtual Desktop is a meticulously structured guide designed to equip IT professionals with the essential knowledge and practical skills required to deploy, manage, and optimize virtual desktop environments within the Microsoft Azure ecosystem. As organizations increasingly adopt cloud-based solutions for remote work and virtual desktop infrastructure (VDI), the need for skilled professionals proficient in Azure Virtual Desktop has grown significantly. This book is aligned with the objectives of the AZ-140 certification exam, covering key topics such as architecture design, deployment strategies, security and compliance considerations, performance optimization, and troubleshooting techniques. Through a methodical approach, each chapter builds upon foundational concepts, gradually advancing to complex configurations and real-world applications, ensuring a well-rounded understanding of Azure Virtual Desktop.

Beyond serving as a certification study resource, Microsoft Azure Virtual Desktop AZ 140: Microsoft Azure Virtual Desktop is a valuable reference for professionals seeking to refine their expertise in virtual desktop solutions. Each chapter integrates practical examples, industry case studies, and self-assessment tools to reinforce learning and enhance retention. Additionally, supplementary resources such as online test papers and expert-led video tutorials provide an immersive learning experience, bridging the gap between theoretical knowledge and hands-on implementation. Whether you are preparing for the AZ-140 exam or looking to advance your career as an Azure Virtual Desktop administrator, this guide offers the structured insights and practical guidance necessary to excel in managing modern cloud-based desktop environments.

Table of Contents

Chapter 1: Practice Questions & Answers Part 1

QUESTION 1: You have the devices shown in the following table.

Name	Operating System
Device 1	Windows 10 Home
Device 2	Windows 8.1 Professional
Device 3	Windows 10 IOT enterprise

You plan to deploy Windows Virtual Desktop for client access to remove virtualized apps. Which devices support the Remote Desktop client?
A. Device1 and Device2 only
B. Device1 and Device3 only
C. Device1, Device2, and De vice3
D. Device1 only
Answer: B

QUESTION 2
You plan to deploy Windows Virtual Desktop.
Users have the devices shown in the following table.

Type	Platform
Tablet	Windows 10 Pro
Phone	Android
Laptop	macOS

From which device types can the users connect to Windows Virtual Desktop resources by using the Remote Desktop client app and the Remote Desktop web client? To answer, select the appropriate options in the answer area.
NOTE: Each correct selection is worth one point.
A. Mastered
B. Not Mastered
Answer: A

QUESTION 3
Your company has a main office and two branch offices. Each office connects directly to the internet. The router in each branch office is configured as an endpoint for the following VPNs:
A VPN connection to the main office A site-to-site VPN to Azure
The routers in each branch office have the Quality of Service (QoS) rules shown in the following table.

Name	Destination	Available Bandwidth allocated
Rule 1	VPN traffic to the main office	25%
Rule 2	Site-to-site VPN traffic to all Azure and Microsoft 365 public IP addresses.	25%
Rule 3	HTTP/HTTPS traffic to all Azure and Microsoft 365 public IP addresses.	25%
Rule 4	Traffic to non-Microsoft internet addresses.	25%

Users in the branch office report slow responses and connection errors when they attempt to connect to Windows Virtual Desktop resources. You need to modify the QoS rules on the branch office routers to improve Windows Virtual Desktop performance.

For which rule should you increase the bandwidth allocation?

A. Rule2
B. Rule3
C. Rule4
D. Rule1

Answer: B

QUESTION 4

You plan to deploy Windows Virtual Desktop. The deployment will use existing virtual machines.

You create a Windows Virtual Desktop host pool.

You need to ensure that you can add the virtual machines to the host pool. What should you do first?

A. Register the Microsoft.DesktopVirtualization provider.
B. Generate a registration key.
C. Run the Invoke-AzVMRunCommand cmdlet.
D. Create a role assignment.

Answer: A

QUESTION 5

You deploy a Windows Virtual Desktop host pool named Pool1.

You have an Azure Storage account named store1 that stores FSLogix profile containers in a share named profiles. You need to configure the path to the storage containers for the session hosts.

Which path should you use?

A. \\store1.blob.core.windows.net\profiles
B. https://store1.file.core.windows.net/profiles
C. \\store1.file.core.windows.net\profiles
D. https://store1.blob.core.windows.net/profiles

Answer: C

QUESTION 6

Note: This question is part of a series of questions that present the same scenario. Each question in the series contains a unique solution that might meet the stated goals. Some question sets might have more than one correct solution, while others might not have a correct solution.
After you answer a question in this section, you will NOT be able to return to it. As a result, these questions will not appear in the review screen. You have a Windows Virtual Desktop host pool that contains five session hosts. The session hosts run Windows 10 Enterprise multi-session.
You need to prevent users from accessing the internet from Windows Virtual Desktop sessions. The session hosts must be allowed to access all the required Microsoft services. Solution: You configure rules in the network security group (NSG) linked to the subnet of the session hosts.
Does that meet the goal?

A. Yes
B. No
Answer: A

QUESTION 7
Note: This question is part of a series of questions that present the same scenario. Each question in the series contains a unique solution that might meet the stated goals. Some question sets might have more than one correct solution, while others might not have a correct solution.
After you answer a question in this section, you will NOT be able to return to it. As a result, these questions will not appear in the review screen.
You have a Windows Virtual Desktop host pool named Pool1 that is integrated with an Azure Active Directory Domain Services (Azure AD DS) managed domain. You need to configure idle session timeout settings for users that connect to the session hosts in Pool1. Solution: From an Azure AD DS-joined computer, you modify the AADDC Users GPO settings.
Does that meet the goal?

A. Yes
B. No
Answer: B

QUESTION 8
Note: This question is part of a series of questions that present the same scenario. Each question in the series contains a unique solution that might meet the stated goals. Some question sets might have more than one correct solution, while others might not have a correct solution.
After you answer a question in this section, you will NOT be able to return to it. As a result, these questions will not appear in the review screen.
You have a Windows Virtual Desktop host pool named Pool1 that is integrated with an Azure Active Directory Domain Services (Azure AD DS) managed domain. You need to configure idle session timeout settings for users that connect to the session hosts in Pool1.
Solution: From an Azure AD DS-joined computer, you modify the AADDC Computers GPO settings. Does that meet the goal?

A. Yes
B. No
Answer: A

QUESTION 11

You have a Windows Virtual Desktop deployment. You publish a RemoteApp named AppVersion1.

You need AppVersion1 to appear in the Remote Desktop client as Sales Contact Application. Which PowerShell cmdlet should you use?

A. New-AzADApplication
B. Update-AzWvdApplicationGroup
C. Register-AzWvdApplicationGroup
D. Update-AzWvdApplication
Answer: D

QUESTION 12

You network contains an on-premises Active Directory domain. The domain contains a universal security group named WVDusers. You have a hybrid Azure Active Directory (Azure AD) tenant. WVDusers syncs to Azure AD.

You have a Windows Virtual Desktop host pool that contains four Windows 10 Enterprise multi-session hosts.

You need to ensure that only the members of WVDusers can establish Windows Virtual Desktop sessions to the host pool. What should you do?

A. Assign WVDusers to an Azure role scoped to each host pool.
B. On each session host, add WVDusers to the local Remote Desktop Users group.
C. Assign WVDusers to an Azure role scoped to the session hosts.
D. Assign WVDusers to an application group.
Answer: D

QUESTION 13

You deploy multiple Windows Virtual Desktop session hosts that have only private IP addresses. You need to ensure that administrators can initiate an RDP session to the session hosts by using the Azure portal. What should you implement?

A. Remote Desktop Connection Broker (RD Connection Broker)
B. Azure Application Gateway
C. Azure Bastion
D. Remote Desktop Session Host (RD Session Host)
Answer: C

QUESTION 14

You have a Windows Virtual Desktop host pool named Pool1 and an Azure Automation account named account1. Pool1 is integrated with an Azure Active Directory Domain Services (Azure AD DS) managed domain named contoso.com.

You plan to configure scaling for Pool1 by using Azure Automation runbooks.

You need to authorize the runbooks to manage the scaling of Pool1. The solution must minimize administrative effort. What should you configure?

A. a managed identity in Azure Active Directory (Azure AD)
B. a group Managed Service Account (gMSA) in Azure AD DS
C. a Connections shared resource in Azure Automation
D. a Run As account in Azure Automation
Answer: D

QUESTION 15
You have an Azure subscription that contains the resources shown in the following table.

Name	Description
WVDVM-0	A virtual machine used in a pooled virtual machine set.
Share 1	An Azure file share that stores FSLogix profile containers.
Image 1	A custom windows 10 image in a shared image gallery.
Image2	A custom windows Server 2019 image stored in Azure Blob Storage.

Which resources can you back up by using Azure Backup?
A. WVDVM-0 and share1 only
B. WVDVM-0 only
C. WVDVM-0, Image1, and Image2 only
D. WVDVM-0, share1, and Image1 only
E. WVDVM-0, share1, Image1, and Image2
Answer: A

QUESTION 16
You plan to implement the FSLogix profile containers for the Seattle office. Which storage account should you use?

A. storage2
B. storage4
C. storage3
D. storage1
Answer: A

QUESTION 17
Which two roles should you assign to Admin1 to meet the security requirements? Each correct answer presents part of the solution. NOTE: Each correct selection is worth one point.

A. Desktop Virtualization Host Pool Contributor
B. Desktop Virtualization Application Group Contributor
C. Desktop Virtualization Workspace Contributor
D. Desktop Virtualization Application Group Reader
E. User Access Administrator

Answer: BC

QUESTION 18
You have the devices shown in the following table.
You plan to deploy Windows Virtual Desktop for client access to remove virtualized apps. Which devices support the Remote Desktop client?

A. Device1 and Device2 only
B. Device1 and Device3 only
C. Device1, Device2, and Device3
D. Device1 only
Answer: B

QUESTION 19

You have a Windows Virtual Desktop host pool that has a max session limit of 15. Disconnected sessions are signed out immediately. The session hosts for the host pool are shown in the following exhibit.

Use the drop-down menus to select the answer choice that completes each statement based on the information presented in the graphic. NOTE: Each correct selection is worth one point.
A. Mastered
B. Not Mastered
Answer: A

QUESTION 20
You have an Azure virtual machine named VM1 that runs Windows 10 Enterprise multi-session.
You plan to add language packs to VM1 and create a custom image of VM1 for a Windows Virtual Desktop host pool.
You need to ensure that modern apps can use the additional language packs when you deploy session hosts by using the custom image. Which command should you run first? To answer, select the appropriate options in the answer area.
NOTE: Each correct selection is worth one point. Hot Area:
A. Mastered
B. Not Mastered
Answer: A

QUESTION 21
You have a shared image gallery that contains the Windows 10 images shown in the following table.
You create a Windows Virtual Desktop deployment that has the following settings:
Host pool name: Pool1 Location: West US
Host pool type: Personal
Which images can you use for the session hosts?

A. Image1 only

B. Image1, Image2, Image3, and Image4
C. Image2 only
D. Image1 and Image2 only
E. Image1 and Image3 only
Answer: E

QUESTION 22
DRAG DROP
You plan to deploy Windows Virtual Desktop.
You need to create Azure NetApp Files storage to store FSLogix profile containers.
Which four actions should you perform in sequence after you register the NetApp Resource Provider? To answer, move the appropriate actions from the list of actions to the answer area and arrange them in the correct order.
NOTE: More than one order of answer choices is correct. You will receive credit for any of the correct orders you select.
A. Mastered
B. Not Mastered
Answer: A

QUESTION 23
Note: This question is part of a series of questions that present the same scenario. Each question in the series contains a unique solution that might meet the stated goals. Some question sets might have more than one correct solution, while others might not have a correct solution.
After you answer a question in this section, you will NOT be able to return to it. As a result, these questions will not appear in the review screen. You have a Windows Virtual Desktop host pool that contains five session hosts. The session hosts run Windows 10 Enterprise multi-session.
You need to prevent users from accessing the internet from Windows Virtual Desktop sessions. The session hosts must be allowed to access all the required Microsoft services. Solution: You configure rules in the network security group (NSG) linked to the subnet of the session hosts.
Does that meet the goal?

A. Yes
B. No

Answer: A

QUESTION 24
Note: This question is part of a series of questions that present the same scenario. Each question in the series contains a unique solution that might meet the stated goals. Some question sets might have more than one correct solution, while others might not have a correct solution.
After you answer a question in this section, you will NOT be able to return to it. As a result, these questions will not appear in the review screen. You have a Windows Virtual Desktop host pool that contains five session hosts. The session hosts run Windows 10 Enterprise multi-session.
You need to prevent users from accessing the internet from Windows Virtual Desktop sessions. The session hosts must be allowed to access all the required Microsoft services. Solution: You configure the Address space settings of the virtual network that contains the session hosts.

Does that meet the goal?

A. Yes
B. No
Answer: B

QUESTION 25
Your company has the offices shown in the following table.
QUESTION 26
Note: This question is part of a series of questions that present the same scenario. Each question in the series contains a unique solution that might meet the stated goals. Some question sets might have more than one correct solution, while others might not have a correct solution.
After you answer a question in this section, you will NOT be able to return to it. As a result, these questions will not appear in the review screen.
You have a Windows Virtual Desktop host pool named Pool1 that is integrated with an Azure Active Directory Domain Services (Azure AD DS) managed domain. You need to configure idle session timeout settings for users that connect to the session hosts in Pool1. Solution: From an Azure AD DS-joined computer, you modify the AADDC Users GPO settings.
Does that meet the goal?

A. Yes
B. No
Answer: B

QUESTION 27
Note: This question is part of a series of questions that present the same scenario. Each question in the series contains a unique solution that might meet the stated goals. Some question sets might have more than one correct solution, while others might not have a correct solution.
After you answer a question in this section, you will NOT be able to return to it. As a result, these questions will not appear in the review screen.
You have a Windows Virtual Desktop host pool named Pool1 that is integrated with an Azure Active Directory Domain Services (Azure AD DS) managed domain. You need to configure idle session timeout settings for users that connect to the session hosts in Pool1.
Solution: From the Azure portal, you modify the Session behavior settings in the RDP Properties of Pool1. Does that meet the goal?

A. Yes
B. No
Answer: B

QUESTION 28
You have a Windows Virtual Desktop deployment that contains the following:
A host pool named Pool1
Two session hosts named Host1 and Host2

An application group named RemoteAppGroup1 that contains a RemoteApp named App1 You need to prevent users from copying and pasting between App1 and their local device. What should you do?

A. Create an AppLocker policy.
B. Modify the locks of RemoteAppGroup1.
C. Modify the locks of RemoteAppGroup1.
D. Modify the RDP Properties of Pool1.
Answer: D

QUESTION 29
You have a Windows Virtual Desktop host pool named Pool1.
You are troubleshooting an issue for a Remote Desktop client that stopped responding.
You need to restore the default Remote Desktop client settings and unsubscribe from all workspaces. Which command should you run?

A. msrdcw
B. resetengine
C. mstsc
D. resetpluginhost
Answer: A

QUESTION 30
Your network contains an on-premises Active Directory domain and a Windows Virtual Desktop deployment. The computer accounts for all the session hosts are in an organizational unit (OU) named WVDHostsOU. All user accounts are in an OU named CorpUsers.
A domain administrator creates a Group Policy Object (GPO) named Policy1 that only contains user settings. The administrator links Policy1 to WVDHostsOU. You discover that when users sign in to the session hosts, none of the settings from Policy1 are applied.
What should you configure to apply GPO settings to the users when they sign in to the session hosts?

A. loopback processing
B. FSLogix profiles
C. mandatory Roaming User Profiles
D. restricted groups
Answer: A

QUESTION 31
You have a Windows Virtual Desktop deployment.
You need to provide external users with access to the deployment. The external users have computers that run Windows 10 Pro and Windows 10 Enterprise. The users do not have the ability to install applications. What should you recommend that the users use to connect to the deployment?

A. Microsoft Edge

B. RemoteApp and Desktop Connection
C. Remote Desktop Manager
D. Remote Desktop Connection
Answer: A

QUESTION 32
You network contains an on-premises Active Directory domain. The domain contains a universal security group named WVDusers. You have a hybrid Azure Active Directory (Azure AD) tenant. WVDusers syncs to Azure AD.
You have a Windows Virtual Desktop host pool that contains four Windows 10 Enterprise multi-session hosts.
You need to ensure that only the members of WVDusers can establish Windows Virtual Desktop sessions to the host pool. What should you do?

A. Assign WVDusers to an Azure role scoped to each host pool.
B. On each session host, add WVDusers to the local Remote Desktop Users group.
C. Assign WVDusers to an Azure role scoped to the session hosts.
D. Assign WVDusers to an application group.
Answer: D

QUESTION 33
You have a Windows Virtual Desktop host pool named Pool1 and an Azure Automation account named account1. Pool1 is integrated with an Azure Active Directory Domain Services (Azure AD DS) managed domain named contoso.com.
You plan to configure scaling for Pool1 by using Azure Automation runbooks.
You need to authorize the runbooks to manage the scaling of Pool1. The solution must minimize administrative effort. What should you configure?

A. a managed identity in Azure Active Directory (Azure AD)
B. a group Managed Service Account (gMSA) in Azure AD DS
C. a Connections shared resource in Azure Automation
D. a Run As account in Azure Automation
Answer: D

QUESTION 34
You have a Windows Virtual Desktop host pool named Pool1 that runs Windows 10 Enterprise multi-session hosts.
You need to use Performance Monitor to troubleshoot a low frame quality issue that is affecting a current use session to Pool1. What should you run to retrieve the user session ID?

A. Get-ComputerInfo
B. qwinsta
C. whoami
D. Get-LocalUser
Answer: B

QUESTION 35
You have an Azure subscription that contains the resources shown in the following table.
Which resources can you back up by using Azure Backup?

A. WVDVM-0 and share1 only
B. WVDVM-0 only
C. WVDVM-0, Image1, and Image2 only
D. WVDVM-0, share1, and Image1 only
E. WVDVM-0, share1, Image1, and Image2
Answer: A

QUESTION 36
DRAG DROP
You have a Windows Virtual Desktop host pool named Pool1. Pool1 contains session hosts that use FSLogix profile containers hosted in Azure NetApp Files volumes. You need to back up profile files by using snapshots.
Which three actions should you perform in sequence? To answer, move the appropriate actions from the list of actions to the answer area and arrange them in the correct order.
A. Mastered
B. Not Mastered
Answer: A

QUESTION 37
You plan to implement the FSLogix profile containers for the Seattle office. Which storage account should you use?
A. storage2
B. storage4
C. storage3
D. storage1
Answer: A

QUESTION 38
Which role should you assign to Operator2 to meet the technical requirements?

A. Desktop Virtualization Session Host Operator
B. Desktop Virtualization Host Pool Contributor
C. Desktop Virtualization User Session Operator
D. Desktop Virtualization Contributor

Answer: B

QUESTION 39
Which users can create Pool4, and which users can join session hosts to the domain? To answer, select the appropriate options in the answer area. NOTE: Each correct selection is worth one point.
A. Mastered
B. Not Mastered

Answer: A

QUESTION 40
You need to recommend an authentication solution that meets the performance requirements. Which two actions should you include in the recommendation? Each correct answer presents part of the solution. NOTE: Each correct selection is worth one point.

A. Join all the session hosts to Azure AD.
B. In each Azure region that will contain the Windows Virtual Desktop session hosts, create an Azure Active Directory Domain Service (Azure AD DS) managed domain.
C. Deploy domain controllers for the on-premises Active Directory domain on Azure virtual machines.
D. Deploy read-only domain controllers (RODCs) on Azure virtual machines.
E. In each Azure region that will contain the Windows Virtual Desktop session hosts, create an Active Directory site.
Answer: AC

QUESTION 41
DRAG DROP
You need to ensure that you can implement user profile shares for the Boston office users. The solution must meet the user profile requirements.
Which four actions should you perform in sequence? To answer, move the appropriate actions from the list of actions to the answer area and arrange them in the correct order.
A. Mastered
B. Not Mastered
Answer: A

QUESTION 42
You need to configure the device redirection settings. The solution must meet the technical requirements. Where should you configure the settings?
A. Workspace1
B. MontrealUsers
C. Group1
D. Pool1
Answer: D

QUESTION 43
You have the devices shown in the following table.
You plan to deploy Windows Virtual Desktop for client access to remove virtualized apps. Which devices support the Remote Desktop client?

A. Device1 and Device2 only
B. Device1 and Device3 only
C. Device1, Device2, and Device3
D. Device1 only
Answer: B

QUESTION 44
You plan to deploy Windows Virtual Desktop to meet the department requirements shown in the following table

You plan to use Windows Virtual Desktop host pools with load balancing and autoscaling.
You need to recommend a host pool design that meets the requirements. The solution must minimize costs. What is the minimum number of host pools you should recommend?

A. 1
B. 2
C. 3
D. 4
Answer: C

QUESTION 45
You deploy a Windows Virtual Desktop host pool named Pool1.
You have an Azure Storage account named store1 that stores FSLogix profile containers in a share named profiles. You need to configure the path to the storage containers for the session hosts. Which path should you use?

A. \\store1.blob.core.windows.net\profiles
B. https://store1.file.core.windows.net/profiles
C. \\store1.file.core.windows.net\profiles
D. https://store1.blob.core.windows.net/profiles
Answer: C

QUESTION 46
You have a Windows Virtual Desktop host pool that has a max session limit of 15. Disconnected sessions are signed out immediately. The session hosts for the host pool are shown in the following exhibit.
Use the drop-down menus to select the answer choice that completes each statement based on the information presented in the graphic. NOTE: Each correct selection is worth one point.
A. Mastered
B. Not Mastered
Answer: A

QUESTION 47
You have an Azure subscription that contains the virtual machines shown in the following table.
You create a shared image gallery as shown in the SharedGallery1 exhibit. (Click the SharedGallery1 tab.)
You create an image definition as shown in the Image1 exhibit. (Click the Image1 tab.)
For each of the following statements, select Yes if the statement is true. Otherwise, select No. NOTE: Each correct selection is worth one point.
Hot Area:

A. Mastered
B. Not Mastered
Answer: A

QUESTION 48
You have a Windows Virtual Desktop host pool named Pool1 and an Azure Storage account named Storage1. Storage1 stores FSLogix profile containers in a share folder named share1. You create a new group named Group1. You provide Group1 with permission to sign in to Pool1.
You need to ensure that the members of Group1 can store the FSLogix profile containers in share1. The solution must use the principle of least privilege. Which two privileges should you assign to Group1? Each correct answer presents part of the solution.
NOTE: Each correct selection is worth one point.
A. the Storage Blob Data Contributor role for storage1
B. the List folder / read data NTFS permissions for share1
C. the Modify NTFS permissions for share1
D. the Storage File Data SMB Share Reader role for storage1
E. the Storage File Data SMB Share Elevated Contributor role for storage1
F. the Storage File Data SMB Share Contributor role for storage1
Answer: CF

QUESTION 49
You have a Windows Virtual Desktop host pool.
You need to install Microsoft Antimalware for Azure on the session hosts. What should you do?
A. Add an extension to each session host.
B. From a Group Policy Object (GPO), enable Windows 10 security features.
C. Configure the RDP Properties of the host pool.
D. Sign in to each session host and install a Windows feature.
Answer: A

QUESTION 50
You have a Windows Virtual Desktop deployment.
You need to ensure that all the connections to the managed resources in the host pool require multi-factor authentication (MFA). Which two settings should you modify in a conditional access policy? To answer, select the appropriate options in the answer area. NOTE: Each correct selection is worth one point.
A. Mastered
B. Not Mastered
Answer: A

QUESTION 51
Your company has the offices shown in the following table.
The company has an Azure Active Directory (Azure AD) tenant named contoso.com that contains a user named User1.
Users connect to a Windows Virtual Desktop deployment named WVD1. WVD1 contains session hosts that have public IP addresses from the 52.166.253.0/24 subnet.

Contoso.com has a conditional access policy that has the following settings: Name: Policy1
Assignments:
- Users and groups: User1
Cloud apps or actions: Windows Virtual Desktop Access controls:
Grant: Grant access, Require multi-factor authentication Enable policy: On
For each of the following statements, select Yes if the statement is true. Otherwise, select No.
NOTE: Each correct selection is worth one point.
Hot Area:
A. Mastered
B. Not Mastered
Answer: A

QUESTION 52
Note: This question is part of a series of questions that present the same scenario. Each question in the series contains a unique solution that might meet the stated goals. Some question sets might have more than one correct solution, while others might not have a correct solution.
After you answer a question in this section, you will NOT be able to return to it. As a result, these questions will not appear in the review screen.
You have a Windows Virtual Desktop host pool named Pool1 that is integrated with an Azure Active Directory Domain Services (Azure AD DS) managed domain. You need to configure idle session timeout settings for users that connect to the session hosts in Pool1.
Solution: From an Azure AD DS-joined computer, you modify the AADDC Computers GPO settings. Does that meet the goal?

A. Yes
B. No
Answer: A

QUESTION 53
Note: This question is part of a series of questions that present the same scenario. Each question in the series contains a unique solution that might meet the stated goals. Some question sets might have more than one correct solution, while others might not have a correct solution.
After you answer a question in this section, you will NOT be able to return to it. As a result, these questions will not appear in the review screen.
You have a Windows Virtual Desktop host pool named Pool1 that is integrated with an Azure Active Directory Domain Services (Azure AD DS) managed domain. You need to configure idle session timeout settings for users that connect to the session hosts in Pool1.
Solution: From the Azure portal, you modify the Session behavior settings in the RDP Properties of Pool1. Does that meet the goal?

A. Yes
B. No

Answer: B

QUESTION 54

You have a Windows Virtual Desktop deployment. You publish a RemoteApp named AppVersion1.
You need AppVersion1 to appear in the Remote Desktop client as Sales Contact Application. Which PowerShell cmdlet should you use?

A. New-AzADApplication
B. Update-AzWvdApplicationGroup
C. Register-AzWvdApplicationGroup
D. Update-AzWvdApplication
Answer: D

QUESTION 55
You have a Windows Virtual Desktop deployment that contains the following:
A host pool named Pool1
Two session hosts named Host1 and Host2
An application group named RemoteAppGroup1 that contains a RemoteApp named App1 You need to prevent users from copying and pasting between App1 and their local device. What should you do?

A. Create an AppLocker policy.
B. Modify the locks of RemoteAppGroup1.
C. Modify the locks of RemoteAppGroup1.
D. Modify the RDP Properties of Pool1.
Answer: D

QUESTION 55
You network contains an on-premises Active Directory domain that syncs to an Azure Active Directory (Azure AD) tenant. The domain contains the users shown in the following table.
You have a Windows Virtual Desktop deployment that contains the application groups shown in the following table. You have the workspaces shown in the following table.
For each of the following statements, select Yes if the statement is true. Otherwise, select No. NOTE: Each correct selection is worth one point.
A. Mastered
B. Not Mastered
Answer: A

QUESTION 56
You have a Windows Virtual Desktop host pool that contains two session hosts. The Microsoft Teams client is installed on each session host.
You discover that only the Microsoft Teams chat and collaboration features work. The calling and meeting features are disabled. You need to ensure that users can set the calling and meeting features from within Microsoft Teams.
What should you do?

A. Install the Remote Desktop WebRTC Redirector Service.
B. Configure Remote audio mode in the RDP Properties.

C. Install the Teams Meeting add-in for Outlook.
D. Configure audio input redirection.
Answer: A

QUESTION 57
You have a Windows Virtual Desktop host pool that contains 20 Windows 10 Enterprise multi-session hosts.
Users connect to the Windows Virtual Desktop deployment from computers that run Windows 10. You plan to implement FSLogix Application Masking. You need to deploy Application Masking rule sets. The solution must minimize administrative effort. To where should you copy the rule sets?

A. the FSLogix profile container of each user
B. C:\Program Files\FSLogix\Apps\Rules on every Windows 10 computer
C. C:\Program Files\FSLogix\Apps\Rules on every session host
Answer: C

QUESTION 58
You network contains an on-premises Active Directory domain. The domain contains a universal security group named WVDusers. You have a hybrid Azure Active Directory (Azure AD) tenant. WVDusers syncs to Azure AD.
You have a Windows Virtual Desktop host pool that contains four Windows 10 Enterprise multi-session hosts.
You need to ensure that only the members of WVDusers can establish Windows Virtual Desktop sessions to the host pool. What should you do?

A. Assign WVDusers to an Azure role scoped to each host pool.
B. On each session host, add WVDusers to the local Remote Desktop Users group.
C. Assign WVDusers to an Azure role scoped to the session hosts.
D. Assign WVDusers to an application group.
Answer: D

QUESTION 59
You have an Azure subscription that contains the resources shown in the following table.
Which resources can you back up by using Azure Backup?

A. WVDVM-0 and share1 only
B. WVDVM-0 only
C. WVDVM-0, Image1, and Image2 only
D. WVDVM-0, share1, and Image1 only
E. WVDVM-0, share1, Image1, and Image2
Answer: A

QUESTION 60

You are planning the deployment of Pool4.

What will be the maximum number of users that can connect to Pool4, and how many session hosts are needed to support five concurrent user sessions? To answer, select the appropriate options in the answer area.
NOTE: Each correct selection is worth one point.
A. Mastered
B. Not Mastered
Answer: A

QUESTION 61
You plan to implement the FSLogix profile containers for the Seattle office. Which storage account should you use?

A. storage2
B. storage4
C. storage3
D. storage1
Answer: A

QUESTION 62
Which role should you assign to Operator2 to meet the technical requirements?

A. Desktop Virtualization Session Host Operator
B. Desktop Virtualization Host Pool Contributor
C. Desktop Virtualization User Session Operator
D. Desktop Virtualization Contributor
Answer: B

QUESTION 63
You need to recommend an authentication solution that meets the performance requirements. Which two actions should you include in the recommendation? Each correct answer presents part of the solution. NOTE: Each correct selection is worth one point.

A. Join all the session hosts to Azure AD.
B. In each Azure region that will contain the Windows Virtual Desktop session hosts, create an Azure Active Directory Domain Service (Azure AD DS) managed domain.
C. Deploy domain controllers for the on-premises Active Directory domain on Azure virtual machines.
D. Deploy read-only domain controllers (RODCs) on Azure virtual machines.
E. In each Azure region that will contain the Windows Virtual Desktop session hosts, create an Active Directory site.
Answer: AC

QUESTION 64
DRAG DROP
You need to ensure that you can implement user profile shares for the Boston office users. The solution must meet the user profile requirements.

Which four actions should you perform in sequence? To answer, move the appropriate actions from the list of actions to the answer area and arrange them in the correct order.
A. Mastered
B. Not Mastered
Answer: A

QUESTION 45
Which two roles should you assign to Admin1 to meet the security requirements? Each correct answer presents part of the solution. NOTE: Each correct selection is worth one point.

A. Desktop Virtualization Host Pool Contributor
B. Desktop Virtualization Application Group Contributor
C. Desktop Virtualization Workspace Contributor
D. Desktop Virtualization Application Group Reader
E. User Access Administrator
Answer: BC

QUESTION 65
You need to configure the device redirection settings. The solution must meet the technical requirements. Where should you configure the settings?

A. Workspace1
B. MontrealUsers
C. Group1
D. Pool1
Answer: D

QUESTION 66
You need to configure the virtual machines that have the Pool1 prefix. The solution must meet the technical requirements. What should you use?

A. a Windows Virtual Desktop automation task
B. Virtual machine auto-shutdown
C. Service Health in Azure Monitor
D. Azure Automation
Answer: A

QUESTION 67
You have the devices shown in the following table.
You plan to deploy Windows Virtual Desktop for client access to remove virtualized apps. Which devices support the Remote Desktop client?

A. Device1 and Device2 only
B. Device1 and Device3 only
C. Device1, Device2, and Device3
D. Device1 only

Answer: B

QUESTION 68
You have a Windows Virtual Desktop host pool that has a max session limit of 15. Disconnected sessions are signed out immediately. The session hosts for the host pool are shown in the following exhibit.

Use the drop-down menus to select the answer choice that completes each statement based on the information presented in the graphic. NOTE: Each correct selection is worth one point.
A. Mastered
B. Not Mastered
Answer: A

QUESTION 69
You have an Azure virtual machine named VM1 that runs Windows 10 Enterprise multi-session.
You plan to add language packs to VM1 and create a custom image of VM1 for a Windows Virtual Desktop host pool.
You need to ensure that modern apps can use the additional language packs when you deploy session hosts by using the custom image. Which command should you run first? To answer, select the appropriate options in the answer area.
NOTE: Each correct selection is worth one point. Hot Area:
A. Mastered
B. Not Mastered
Answer: A

QUESTION 70
You have a shared image gallery that contains the Windows 10 images shown in the following table.
You create a Windows Virtual Desktop deployment that has the following settings:
Host pool name: Pool1 Location: West US
Host pool type: Personal
Which images can you use for the session hosts?

A. Image1 only
B. Image1, Image2, Image3, and Image4
C. Image2 only
D. Image1 and Image2 only
E. Image1 and Image3 only
Answer: E

QUESTION 71
DRAG DROP
You plan to deploy Windows Virtual Desktop.
You need to create Azure NetApp Files storage to store FSLogix profile containers.

Which four actions should you perform in sequence after you register the NetApp Resource Provider? To answer, move the appropriate actions from the list of actions to the answer area and arrange them in the correct order.
NOTE: More than one order of answer choices is correct. You will receive credit for any of the correct orders you select.
A. Mastered
B. Not Mastered
Answer: A

QUESTION 72
Note: This question is part of a series of questions that present the same scenario. Each question in the series contains a unique solution that might meet the stated goals. Some question sets might have more than one correct solution, while others might not have a correct solution.
After you answer a question in this section, you will NOT be able to return to it. As a result, these questions will not appear in the review screen. You have a Windows Virtual Desktop host pool that contains five session hosts. The session hosts run Windows 10 Enterprise multi-session.
You need to prevent users from accessing the internet from Windows Virtual Desktop sessions. The session hosts must be allowed to access all the required Microsoft services. Solution: You configure rules in the network security group (NSG) linked to the subnet of the session hosts.
Does that meet the goal?

A. Yes
B. No
Answer: A

QUESTION 73
Note: This question is part of a series of questions that present the same scenario. Each question in the series contains a unique solution that might meet the stated goals. Some question sets might have more than one correct solution, while others might not have a correct solution.
After you answer a question in this section, you will NOT be able to return to it. As a result, these questions will not appear in the review screen. You have a Windows Virtual Desktop host pool that contains five session hosts. The session hosts run Windows 10 Enterprise multi-session.
You need to prevent users from accessing the internet from Windows Virtual Desktop sessions. The session hosts must be allowed to access all the required Microsoft services. Solution: You configure the Address space settings of the virtual network that contains the session hosts.
Does that meet the goal?

A. Yes
B. No
Answer: B

QUESTION 74
Your company has the offices shown in the following table.
The company has an Azure Active Directory (Azure AD) tenant named contoso.com that contains a user named User1.

Users connect to a Windows Virtual Desktop deployment named WVD1. WVD1 contains session hosts that have public IP addresses from the 52.166.253.0/24 subnet.
Contoso.com has a conditional access policy that has the following settings: Name: Policy1
Assignments:
- Users and groups: User1
Cloud apps or actions: Windows Virtual Desktop Access controls:
Grant: Grant access, Require multi-factor authentication Enable policy: On
For each of the following statements, select Yes if the statement is true. Otherwise, select No.
NOTE: Each correct selection is worth one point.
Hot Area:
A. Mastered
B. Not Mastered
Answer: A

QUESTION 75
Note: This question is part of a series of questions that present the same scenario. Each question in the series contains a unique solution that might meet the stated goals. Some question sets might have more than one correct solution, while others might not have a correct solution.
After you answer a question in this section, you will NOT be able to return to it. As a result, these questions will not appear in the review screen.
You have a Windows Virtual Desktop host pool named Pool1 that is integrated with an Azure Active Directory Domain Services (Azure AD DS) managed domain. You need to configure idle session timeout settings for users that connect to the session hosts in Pool1. Solution: From an Azure AD DS-joined computer, you modify the AADDC Users GPO settings.
Does that meet the goal?

A. Yes
B. No
Answer: B

QUESTION 76
Note: This question is part of a series of questions that present the same scenario. Each question in the series contains a unique solution that might meet the stated goals. Some question sets might have more than one correct solution, while others might not have a correct solution.
After you answer a question in this section, you will NOT be able to return to it. As a result, these questions will not appear in the review screen.
You have a Windows Virtual Desktop host pool named Pool1 that is integrated with an Azure Active Directory Domain Services (Azure AD DS) managed domain. You need to configure idle session timeout settings for users that connect to the session hosts in Pool1.
Solution: From the Azure portal, you modify the Session behavior settings in the RDP Properties of Pool1. Does that meet the goal?

A. Yes
B. No
Answer: B

QUESTION 77
You have a Windows Virtual Desktop deployment that contains the following:
A host pool named Pool1
Two session hosts named Host1 and Host2
An application group named RemoteAppGroup1 that contains a RemoteApp named App1 You need to prevent users from copying and pasting between App1 and their local device. What should you do?

A. Create an AppLocker policy.
B. Modify the locks of RemoteAppGroup1.
C. Modify the locks of RemoteAppGroup1.
D. Modify the RDP Properties of Pool1.
Answer D

QUESTION 78
You have a Windows Virtual Desktop host pool named Pool1.
You are troubleshooting an issue for a Remote Desktop client that stopped responding.
You need to restore the default Remote Desktop client settings and unsubscribe from all workspaces. Which command should you run?

A. msrdcw
B. resetengine
C. mstsc
D. resetpluginhost
Answer: A

QUESTION 79
Your network contains an on-premises Active Directory domain and a Windows Virtual Desktop deployment. The computer accounts for all the session hosts are in an organizational unit (OU) named WVDHostsOU. All user accounts are in an OU named CorpUsers.
A domain administrator creates a Group Policy Object (GPO) named Policy1 that only contains user settings. The administrator links Policy1 to WVDHostsOU. You discover that when users sign in to the session hosts, none of the settings from Policy1 are applied.
What should you configure to apply GPO settings to the users when they sign in to the session hosts?

A. loopback processing
B. FSLogix profiles
C. mandatory Roaming User Profiles
D. restricted groups
Answer: A

QUESTION 80
You have a Windows Virtual Desktop deployment.
You need to provide external users with access to the deployment. The external users have computers that run Windows 10 Pro and Windows 10 Enterprise. The users do not have the ability

to install applications. What should you recommend that the users use to connect to the deployment?

A. Microsoft Edge
B. RemoteApp and Desktop Connection
C. Remote Desktop Manager
D. Remote Desktop Connection
Answer: A

QUESTION 81
You network contains an on-premises Active Directory domain. The domain contains a universal security group named WVDusers. You have a hybrid Azure Active Directory (Azure AD) tenant. WVDusers syncs to Azure AD.
You have a Windows Virtual Desktop host pool that contains four Windows 10 Enterprise multi-session hosts.
You need to ensure that only the members of WVDusers can establish Windows Virtual Desktop sessions to the host pool. What should you do?

A. Assign WVDusers to an Azure role scoped to each host pool.
B. On each session host, add WVDusers to the local Remote Desktop Users group.
C. Assign WVDusers to an Azure role scoped to the session hosts.
D. Assign WVDusers to an application group.
Answer: D

QUESTION 82
You have a Windows Virtual Desktop host pool named Pool1 and an Azure Automation account named account1. Pool1 is integrated with an Azure Active Directory Domain Services (Azure AD DS) managed domain named contoso.com.
You plan to configure scaling for Pool1 by using Azure Automation runbooks.
You need to authorize the runbooks to manage the scaling of Pool1. The solution must minimize administrative effort. What should you configure?

A. a managed identity in Azure Active Directory (Azure AD)
B. a group Managed Service Account (gMSA) in Azure AD DS
C. a Connections shared resource in Azure Automation
D. a Run As account in Azure Automation
Answer: D

QUESTION 83
You have a Windows Virtual Desktop host pool named Pool1 that runs Windows 10 Enterprise multi-session hosts.
You need to use Performance Monitor to troubleshoot a low frame quality issue that is affecting a current use session to Pool1. What should you run to retrieve the user session ID?

A. Get-ComputerInfo
B. qwinsta

C. whoami
D. Get-LocalUser
Answer: B

QUESTION 84
You have an Azure subscription that contains the resources shown in the following table.
Which resources can you back up by using Azure Backup?

A. WVDVM-0 and share1 only
B. WVDVM-0 only
C. WVDVM-0, Image1, and Image2 only
D. WVDVM-0, share1, and Image1 only
E. WVDVM-0, share1, Image1, and Image2
Answer: A

QUESTION 85
DRAG DROP
You have a Windows Virtual Desktop host pool named Pool1. Pool1 contains session hosts that use FSLogix profile containers hosted in Azure NetApp Files volumes. You need to back up profile files by using snapshots.
Which three actions should you perform in sequence? To answer, move the appropriate actions from the list of actions to the answer area and arrange them in the correct order.

A. Mastered
B. Not Mastered
Answer: A

QUESTION 86
You plan to implement the FSLogix profile containers for the Seattle office. Which storage account should you use?
A. storage2
B. storage4
C. storage3
D. storage1
Answer: A

QUESTION 87
Which role should you assign to Operator2 to meet the technical requirements?

A. Desktop Virtualization Session Host Operator
B. Desktop Virtualization Host Pool Contributor
C. Desktop Virtualization User Session Operator
D. Desktop Virtualization Contributor
Answer: B

QUESTION 88
Which users can create Pool4, and which users can join session hosts to the domain? To answer, select the appropriate options in the answer area. NOTE: Each correct selection is worth one point.
A. Mastered
B. Not Mastered
Answer: A

QUESTION 89
You need to recommend an authentication solution that meets the performance requirements. Which two actions should you include in the recommendation? Each correct answer presents part of the solution. NOTE: Each correct selection is worth one point.

A. Join all the session hosts to Azure AD.
B. In each Azure region that will contain the Windows Virtual Desktop session hosts, create an Azure Active Directory Domain Service (Azure AD DS) managed domain.
C. Deploy domain controllers for the on-premises Active Directory domain on Azure virtual machines.
D. Deploy read-only domain controllers (RODCs) on Azure virtual machines.
E. In each Azure region that will contain the Windows Virtual Desktop session hosts, create an Active Directory site.
Answer: AC

QUESTION 90
DRAG DROP
You need to ensure that you can implement user profile shares for the Boston office users. The solution must meet the user profile requirements.
Which four actions should you perform in sequence? To answer, move the appropriate actions from the list of actions to the answer area and arrange them in the correct order.
A. Mastered
B. Not Mastered
Answer: A

QUESTION 91
You need to configure the device redirection settings. The solution must meet the technical requirements. Where should you configure the settings?

A. Workspace1
B. MontrealUsers
C. Group1
D. Pool1

Answer: D

QUESTION 92
You have an Azure Active Directory (Azure AD) tenant named contoso.com and an Azure virtual network named VNET1.

To VNET1, you deploy an Azure Active Directory Domain Services (Azure AD DS) managed domain named litwareinc.com. To VNET1, you plan to deploy a Windows Virtual Desktop host pool named Pool1.
You need to ensure that you can deploy Windows 10 Enterprise host pools to Pool1. What should you do first?

A. Modify the settings of the litwareinc.com DNS zone.
B. Modify the DNS settings of VNET1.
C. Add a custom domain name to contoso.com.
D. Implement Azure AD Connect cloud sync.
Answer: B

QUESTION 93
You plan to deploy Windows Virtual Desktop to meet the department requirements shown in the following table

Department	Required Windows Virtual Desktop resource	Number of users	GPU required
Research	Single-session desktop	10	No
Engineering	Multi-session desktop	50	Yes
IT	Multi-Session desktop	50	No
Finance	RemoteApp	10	No

You plan to use Windows Virtual Desktop host pools with load balancing and autoscaling.
You need to recommend a host pool design that meets the requirements. The solution must minimize costs. What is the minimum number of host pools you should recommend?
A. 1
B. 2
C. 3
D. 4
Answer: C

QUESTION 94
Your company has a main office and two branch offices. Each office connects directly to the internet. The router in each branch office is configured as an endpoint for the following VPNs:
A VPN connection to the main office A site-to-site VPN to Azure
The routers in each branch office have the Quality of Service (QoS) rules shown in the following table.

Name	Destination	Available bandwidth allocated
Rule1	VPN traffic to the main office	25%
Rule2	Site-to-site VPN traffic to Azure	25%
Rule3	HTTP/HTTPS traffic to all azure and Microsoft 365 public IP addresses	25%
Rule4	Traffic to non-Microsoft internet addresses	25%

Users in the branch office report slow responses and connection errors when they attempt to connect to Windows Virtual Desktop resources. You need to modify the QoS rules on the branch office routers to improve Windows Virtual Desktop performance.
For which rule should you increase the bandwidth allocation?
A. Rule2
B. Rule3
C. Rule4
D. Rule1
Answer: B

QUESTION 95
You plan to deploy Windows Virtual Desktop. The deployment will use existing virtual machines. You create a Windows Virtual Desktop host pool.
You need to ensure that you can add the virtual machines to the host pool. What should you do first?
A. Register the Microsoft.DesktopVirtualization provider.
B. Generate a registration key.
C. Run the Invoke-AzVMRunCommand cmdlet.
D. Create a role assignment.
Answer: A

QUESTION 96
You plan to deploy Windows Virtual Desktop session host virtual machines based on a preconfigured master image. The master image will be stored in a shared image. You create a virtual machine named Image1 to use as the master image. You install applications and apply configuration changes to Image1.
You need to ensure that the new session host virtual machines created based on Image1 have unique names and security identifiers. What should you do on Image1 before you add the image to the shared image gallery?
A. At a command prompt, run the set computername command.
B. At a command prompt, run the sysprep command.
C. From PowerShell, run the rename-computer cmdlet.
D. From the lock screen of the Windows device, perform a Windows Autopilot Reset.
Answer: B

QUESTION 97

Note: This question is part of a series of questions that present the same scenario. Each question in the series contains a unique solution that might meet the stated goals. Some question sets might have more than one correct solution, while others might not have a correct solution.
After you answer a question in this section, you will NOT be able to return to it. As a result, these questions will not appear in the review screen. You have a Windows Virtual Desktop host pool that contains five session hosts. The session hosts run Windows 10 Enterprise multi-session.
You need to prevent users from accessing the internet from Windows Virtual Desktop sessions. The session hosts must be allowed to access all the required Microsoft services.
Solution: You modify the IP configuration of each session host. Does that meet the goal?
A. Yes
B. No
Answer: B

QUESTION 98
You have a Windows Virtual Desktop host pool.
You need to install Microsoft Antimalware for Azure on the session hosts. What should you do?
A. Add an extension to each session host.
B. From a Group Policy Object (GPO), enable Windows 10 security features.
C. Configure the RDP Properties of the host pool.
D. Sign in to each session host and install a Windows feature.
Answer: A
QUESTION 99

Your company has the offices shown in the following table.

Location	Internet network IP address space	Public IP address space
Boston	10.10.0.0/16	13.83.131.0/24
Seattle	172.16.0.0/16	92.15.10.0/24

The company has an Azure Active Directory (Azure AD) tenant named contoso.com that contains a user named User1.
Users connect to a Windows Virtual Desktop deployment named WVD1. WVD1 contains session hosts that have public IP addresses from the 52.166.253.0/24 subnet.
Contoso.com has a conditional access policy that has the following settings: Name: Policy1 Assignments:
- Users and groups: User1
- Cloud apps or actions: Windows Virtual Desktop Access controls:
- Grant: Grant access, Require multi-factor authentication Enable policy: On
For each of the following statements, select Yes if the statement is true. Otherwise, select No.
NOTE: Each correct selection is worth one point. Hot Area:

Statements	Yes/No
If user1 connects to windows Virtual Desktop from the office in Boston, User1 is prompted for multi-factor authentication (MFA)	Yes
If User1 connects to windows Virtual Desktop from home, User1 is Prompted for multi-factor authentication (MFA)	Yes
If User1 connects to Microsoft Exchange from a window Virtual Desktop session. User1 is prompted for multi-factor authentication (MFA)	Yes

A. Mastered
B. Not Mastered
Answer: A

QUESTION 100
Note: This question is part of a series of questions that present the same scenario. Each question in the series contains a unique solution that might meet the stated goals. Some question sets might have more than one correct solution, while others might not have a correct solution.
After you answer a question in this section, you will NOT be able to return to it. As a result, these questions will not appear in the review screen.
You have a Windows Virtual Desktop host pool named Pool1 that is integrated with an Azure Active Directory Domain Services (Azure AD DS) managed domain. You need to configure idle session timeout settings for users that connect to the session hosts in Pool1.
Solution: From an Azure AD DS-joined computer, you modify the AADDC Computers GPO settings. Does that meet the goal?
A. Yes
B. No
Answer: A

QUESTION 101
Note: This question is part of a series of questions that present the same scenario. Each question in the series contains a unique solution that might meet the stated goals. Some question sets might have more than one correct solution, while others might not have a correct solution.
After you answer a question in this section, you will NOT be able to return to it. As a result, these questions will not appear in the review screen.
You have a Windows Virtual Desktop host pool named Pool1 that is integrated with an Azure Active Directory Domain Services (Azure AD DS) managed domain. You need to configure idle session timeout settings for users that connect to the session hosts in Pool1.
Solution: From the Azure portal, you modify the Session behavior settings in the RDP Properties of Pool1. Does that meet the goal?
A. Yes
B. No
Answer: B

QUESTION 102

You network contains an on-premises Active Directory domain that syncs to an Azure Active Directory (Azure AD) tenant. The domain contains the users shown in the following table.

Name	Role	Member of
User1	Desktop Virtualization Workspace Reader	Group1
User2	Desktop Virtualization Application Group	Group2

You have a Windows Virtual Desktop deployment that contains the application groups shown in the following table.

Name	Application	Assignment
AppGroup1	Microsoft word	Group1
AppGroup2	Microsoft Excel	Group2
AppGroup3	Microsoft Power Point	Group1, Group2

You have the workspaces shown in the following table.

Name	Application group
Workspace1	AppGroup1
Workspace2	Appgroup2

For each of the following statements, select Yes if the statement is true. Otherwise, select No.
NOTE: Each correct selection is worth one point.

A. Mastered

B. Not Mastered

Answer: A

QUESTION 103

You have a Windows Virtual Desktop host pool that contains 20 Windows 10 Enterprise multi-session hosts.

Users connect to the Windows Virtual Desktop deployment from computers that run Windows 10.

You plan to implement FSLogix Application Masking. You need to deploy Application Masking rule sets. The solution must minimize administrative effort. To where should you copy the rule sets?

A. the FSLogix profile container of each user

B. C:\Program Files\FSLogix\Apps\Rules on every Windows 10 computer

C. C:\Program Files\FSLogix\Apps\Rules on every session host

Answer: C

QUESTION 104

You have a Windows Virtual Desktop deployment.
You need to provide external users with access to the deployment. The external users have computers that run Windows 10 Pro and Windows 10 Enterprise. The users do not have the ability to install applications. What should you recommend that the users use to connect to the deployment?

A. Microsoft Edge
B. RemoteApp and Desktop Connection
C. Remote Desktop Manager
D. Remote Desktop Connection
Answer: A

Chapter 2: Practice Questions & Answers Part 2

QUESTION 105
You have a Windows Virtual Desktop host pool that runs Windows 10 Enterprise multi-session.
You need to configure automatic scaling of the host pool to meet the following requirements:
Distribute new user sessions across all running session hosts.
Automatically start a new session host when concurrent user sessions exceed 30 users per host.
What should you include in the solution?

A. an Azure Automation account and the depth-first load balancing algorithm
B. an Azure Automation account and the breadth-first load balancing algorithm
C. an Azure load balancer and the breadth-first load balancing algorithm
D. an Azure load balancer and the depth-first load balancing algorithm
Answer: B

QUESTION 106
You have a Windows Virtual Desktop host pool named Pool1 and an Azure Automation account named account1. Pool1 is integrated with an Azure Active Directory Domain Services (Azure AD DS) managed domain named contoso.com.
You plan to configure scaling for Pool1 by using Azure Automation runbooks.
You need to authorize the runbooks to manage the scaling of Pool1. The solution must minimize administrative effort. What should you configure?

A. a managed identity in Azure Active Directory (Azure AD)
B. a group Managed Service Account (gMSA) in Azure AD DS
C. a Connections shared resource in Azure Automation
D. a Run As account in Azure Automation
Answer: D

QUESTION 107
You have a Windows Virtual Desktop host pool named Pool1 that runs Windows 10 Enterprise multi-session hosts.

You need to use Performance Monitor to troubleshoot a low frame quality issue that is affecting a current use session to Pool1. What should you run to retrieve the user session ID?

A. Get-ComputerInfo
B. qwinsta
C. whoami
D. Get-LocalUser
Answer: B

QUESTION 108
You plan to implement the FSLogix profile containers for the Seattle office. Which storage account should you use?

A. storage2
B. storage4
C. storage3
D. storage1
Answer: A

QUESTION 109
You need to ensure the resiliency of the user profiles for the Boston office users. The solution must meet the user performance requirements. What should you do?

A. Modify the Account kind setting of storage1.
B. Modify the replication settings of storage1.
C. Implement Azure Site Recovery.
D. Configure Cloud Cache.
Answer: D

QUESTION 110
You have the devices shown in the following table.

Name	Operating System
Device 1	Windows 10 Home
Device2	Windows 8.1 Professional
Device3	Windows 10 IOT enterprise

You plan to deploy Windows Virtual Desktop for client access to remove virtualized apps. Which devices support the Remote Desktop client?

A. Device1 and Device2 only
B. Device1 and Device3 only
C. Device1, Device2, and Device3
D. Device1 only

Answer: B

QUESTION 111

You plan to deploy Windows Virtual Desktop.
Users have the devices shown in the following table.

Type	Platform
Tablet	Windows 10 Pro
Phone	Android
Laptop	macOS

From which device types can the users connect to Windows Virtual Desktop resources by using the Remote Desktop client app and the Remote Desktop web client? To answer, select the appropriate options in the answer area.
NOTE: Each correct selection is worth one point.
A. Mastered
B. Not Mastered
Answer: A

QUESTION 112
Your company has a main office and two branch offices. Each office connects directly to the internet. The router in each branch office is configured as an endpoint for the following VPNs:
A VPN connection to the main office A site-to-site VPN to Azure
The routers in each branch office have the Quality of Service (QoS) rules shown in the following table.

Name	Destination	Available Bandwidth allocated
Rule1	VPN traffic to the main office	25%
Rule2	Site-to-site VPN traffic to Azure	25%
Rule3	HTTP/HTTPS traffic to all azure and Microsoft 365 public IP addresses.	25%
Rule4	Traffic to non-Microsoft internet addresses	25%

Users in the branch office report slow responses and connection errors when they attempt to connect to Windows Virtual Desktop resources. You need to modify the QoS rules on the branch office routers to improve Windows Virtual Desktop performance.
For which rule should you increase the bandwidth allocation?

A. Rule2
B. Rule3

C. Rule4
D. Rule1
Answer: B

QUESTION 113
You plan to deploy Windows Virtual Desktop. The deployment will use existing virtual machines. You create a Windows Virtual Desktop host pool.
You need to ensure that you can add the virtual machines to the host pool. What should you do first?

A. Register the Microsoft.DesktopVirtualization provider.
B. Generate a registration key.
C. Run the Invoke-AzVMRunCommand cmdlet.
D. Create a role assignment.
Answer: A

QUESTION 114
You deploy a Windows Virtual Desktop host pool named Pool1.
You have an Azure Storage account named store1 that stores FSLogix profile containers in a share named profiles. You need to configure the path to the storage containers for the session hosts. Which path should you use?

A. \\store1.blob.core.windows.net\profiles
B. https://store1.file.core.windows.net/profiles
C. \\store1.file.core.windows.net\profiles
D. https://store1.blob.core.windows.net/profiles
Answer: C

QUESTION 115
You have an Azure virtual machine named VM1 that runs Windows 10 Enterprise multi-session. You plan to add language packs to VM1 and create a custom image of VM1 for a Windows Virtual Desktop host pool.
You need to ensure that modern apps can use the additional language packs when you deploy session hosts by using the custom image. Which command should you run first? To answer, select the appropriate options in the answer area.
NOTE: Each correct selection is worth one point. Hot Area:
A. Mastered
B. Not Mastered
Answer: A

QUESTION 116
DRAG DROP
You have a Windows Virtual Desktop deployment.
You have a session host named Host1 that has the disk layout shown in the exhibit. (Click the Exhibit tab.)

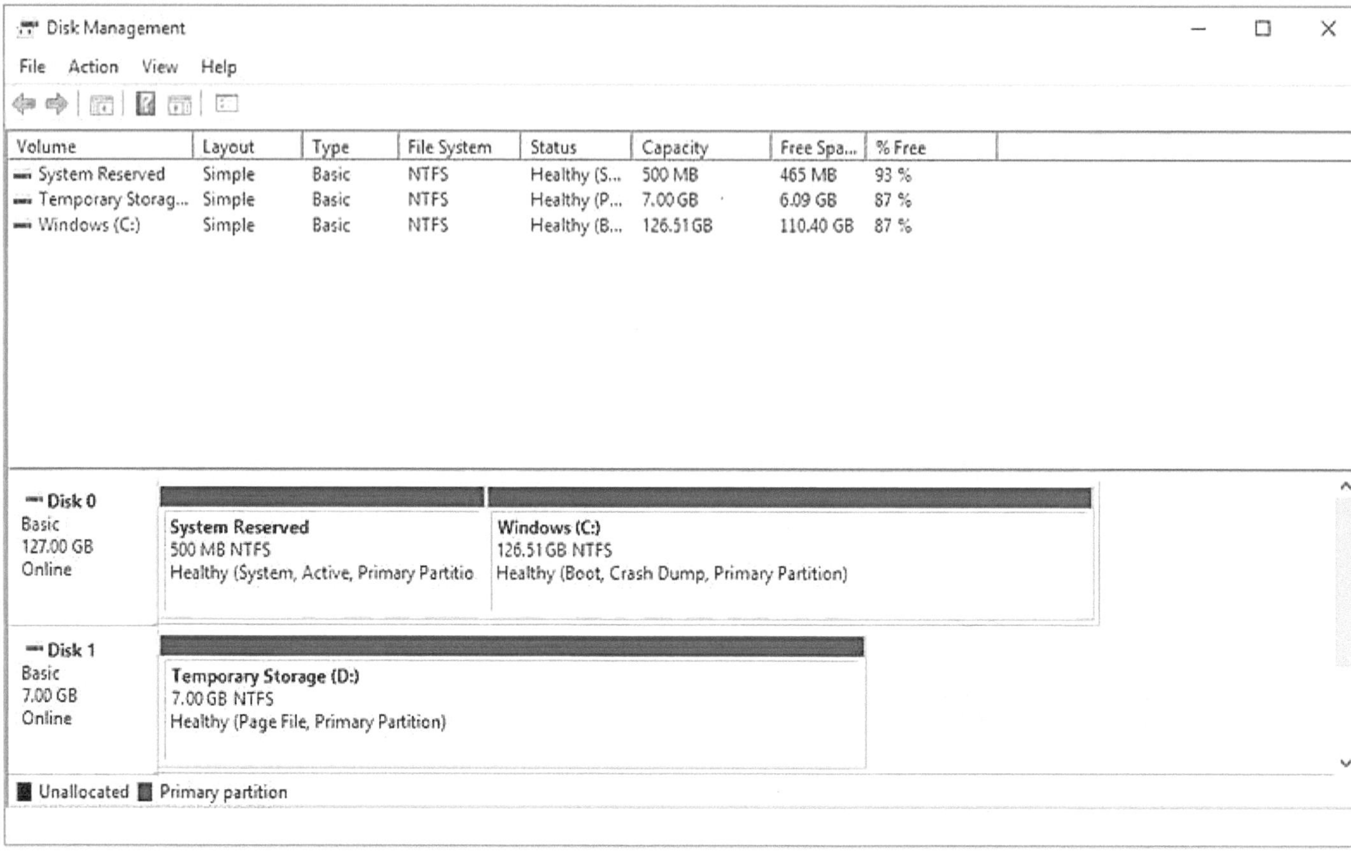

You plan to deploy an app that must be installed on D. The app requires 500 GB of disk space. You need to add a new data disk that will be assigned the drive letter D. The solution must maintain the current performance of Host1.

Which four actions should you perform in sequence? To answer, move the appropriate actions from the list of actions to the answer area and arrange them in the correct order.

Actions	Answer Area
Move the page file to drive C.	
Move the page file to Temporary Storage.	
Change the drive letter of Temporary Storage (D).	
Mark Temporary Storage(D) as Active.	
Add the new disk and assign drive D.	
Move the page file to system Reserved.	

A. Mastered

B. Not Mastered

Answer: A

QUESTION 117

Note: This question is part of a series of questions that present the same scenario. Each question in the series contains a unique solution that might meet the stated goals. Some question sets might have more than one correct solution, while others might not have a correct solution.
After you answer a question in this section, you will NOT be able to return to it. As a result, these questions will not appear in the review screen. You have a Windows Virtual Desktop host pool that contains five session hosts. The session hosts run Windows 10 Enterprise multi-session.
You need to prevent users from accessing the internet from Windows Virtual Desktop sessions. The session hosts must be allowed to access all the required Microsoft services. Solution: You configure rules in the network security group (NSG) linked to the subnet of the session hosts.
Does that meet the goal?

A. Yes
B. No
Answer: A

QUESTION 118
Note: This question is part of a series of questions that present the same scenario. Each question in the series contains a unique solution that might meet the stated goals. Some question sets might have more than one correct solution, while others might not have a correct solution.
After you answer a question in this section, you will NOT be able to return to it. As a result, these questions will not appear in the review screen.
You have a Windows Virtual Desktop host pool named Pool1 that is integrated with an Azure Active Directory Domain Services (Azure AD DS) managed domain. You need to configure idle session timeout settings for users that connect to the session hosts in Pool1. Solution: From an Azure AD DS-joined computer, you modify the AADDC Users GPO settings.
Does that meet the goal?

A. Yes
B. No
Answer: B

QUESTION 119
Note: This question is part of a series of questions that present the same scenario. Each question in the series contains a unique solution that might meet the stated goals. Some question sets might have more than one correct solution, while others might not have a correct solution.
After you answer a question in this section, you will NOT be able to return to it. As a result, these questions will not appear in the review screen.
You have a Windows Virtual Desktop host pool named Pool1 that is integrated with an Azure Active Directory Domain Services (Azure AD DS) managed domain. You need to configure idle session timeout settings for users that connect to the session hosts in Pool1.
Solution: From an Azure AD DS-joined computer, you modify the AADDC Computers GPO settings. Does that meet the goal?

A. Yes
B. No
Answer: A

QUESTION 120
You have a Windows Virtual Desktop deployment. You publish a RemoteApp named AppVersion1.
You need AppVersion1 to appear in the Remote Desktop client as Sales Contact Application.
Which PowerShell cmdlet should you use?

A. New-AzADApplication
B. Update-AzWvdApplicationGroup
C. Register-AzWvdApplicationGroup
D. Update-AzWvdApplication
Answer: D

QUESTION 121
You network contains an on-premises Active Directory domain. The domain contains a universal security group named WVDusers. You have a hybrid Azure Active Directory (Azure AD) tenant. WVDusers syncs to Azure AD.
You have a Windows Virtual Desktop host pool that contains four Windows 10 Enterprise multi-session hosts.
You need to ensure that only the members of WVDusers can establish Windows Virtual Desktop sessions to the host pool. What should you do?

A. Assign WVDusers to an Azure role scoped to each host pool.
B. On each session host, add WVDusers to the local Remote Desktop Users group.
C. Assign WVDusers to an Azure role scoped to the session hosts.
D. Assign WVDusers to an application group.
Answer: D

QUESTION 122
You deploy multiple Windows Virtual Desktop session hosts that have only private IP addresses.
You need to ensure that administrators can initiate an RDP session to the session hosts by using the Azure portal. What should you implement?

A. Remote Desktop Connection Broker (RD Connection Broker)
B. Azure Application Gateway
C. Azure Bastion
D. Remote Desktop Session Host (RD Session Host)
Answer: C

QUESTION 123
You have a Windows Virtual Desktop host pool named Pool1 and an Azure Automation account named account1. Pool1 is integrated with an Azure Active Directory Domain Services (Azure AD DS) managed domain named contoso.com.
You plan to configure scaling for Pool1 by using Azure Automation runbooks.
You need to authorize the runbooks to manage the scaling of Pool1. The solution must minimize administrative effort. What should you configure?

A. a managed identity in Azure Active Directory (Azure AD)
B. a group Managed Service Account (gMSA) in Azure AD DS
C. a Connections shared resource in Azure Automation
D. a Run As account in Azure Automation
Answer: D

QUESTION 124
Which two roles should you assign to Admin1 to meet the security requirements? Each correct answer presents part of the solution. NOTE: Each correct selection is worth one point.

A. Desktop Virtualization Host Pool Contributor
B. Desktop Virtualization Application Group Contributor
C. Desktop Virtualization Workspace Contributor
D. Desktop Virtualization Application Group Reader
E. User Access Administrator
Answer: BC

QUESTION 125
You have the devices shown in the following table.
You plan to deploy Windows Virtual Desktop for client access to remove virtualized apps. Which devices support the Remote Desktop client?

A. Device1 and Device2 only
B. Device1 and Device3 only
C. Device1, Device2, and Device3
D. Device1 only
Answer: B

QUESTION 126
You have a Windows Virtual Desktop host pool that has a max session limit of 15. Disconnected sessions are signed out immediately. The session hosts for the host pool are shown in the following exhibit.

Use the drop-down menus to select the answer choice that completes each statement based on the information presented in the graphic. NOTE: Each correct selection is worth one point.
A. Mastered
B. Not Mastered
Answer: A
QUESTION 127
You have an Azure virtual machine named VM1 that runs Windows 10 Enterprise multi-session.
You plan to add language packs to VM1 and create a custom image of VM1 for a Windows Virtual Desktop host pool.
You need to ensure that modern apps can use the additional language packs when you deploy session hosts by using the custom image. Which command should you run first? To answer, select the appropriate options in the answer area.

NOTE: Each correct selection is worth one point. Hot Area:
A. Mastered
B. Not Mastered
Answer: A

QUESTION 128
You have a shared image gallery that contains the Windows 10 images shown in the following table.
You create a Windows Virtual Desktop deployment that has the following settings:
Host pool name: Pool1 Location: West US
Host pool type: Personal
Which images can you use for the session hosts?

A. Image1 only
B. Image1, Image2, Image3, and Image4
C. Image2 only
D. Image1 and Image2 only
E. Image1 and Image3 only
Answer: E

QUESTION 129
DRAG DROP
You plan to deploy Windows Virtual Desktop.
You need to create Azure NetApp Files storage to store FSLogix profile containers.
Which four actions should you perform in sequence after you register the NetApp Resource Provider? To answer, move the appropriate actions from the list of actions to the answer area and arrange them in the correct order.
NOTE: More than one order of answer choices is correct. You will receive credit for any of the correct orders you select.
A. Mastered
B. Not Mastered
Answer: A

QUESTION 130
Note: This question is part of a series of questions that present the same scenario. Each question in the series contains a unique solution that might meet the stated goals. Some question sets might have more than one correct solution, while others might not have a correct solution.
After you answer a question in this section, you will NOT be able to return to it. As a result, these questions will not appear in the review screen. You have a Windows Virtual Desktop host pool that contains five session hosts. The session hosts run Windows 10 Enterprise multi-session.
You need to prevent users from accessing the internet from Windows Virtual Desktop sessions. The session hosts must be allowed to access all the required Microsoft services. Solution: You configure rules in the network security group (NSG) linked to the subnet of the session hosts.
Does that meet the goal?

A. Yes

B. No
Answer: A

QUESTION 131
Note: This question is part of a series of questions that present the same scenario. Each question in the series contains a unique solution that might meet the stated goals. Some question sets might have more than one correct solution, while others might not have a correct solution.
After you answer a question in this section, you will NOT be able to return to it. As a result, these questions will not appear in the review screen. You have a Windows Virtual Desktop host pool that contains five session hosts. The session hosts run Windows 10 Enterprise multi-session.
You need to prevent users from accessing the internet from Windows Virtual Desktop sessions. The session hosts must be allowed to access all the required Microsoft services. Solution: You configure the Address space settings of the virtual network that contains the session hosts.
Does that meet the goal?
A. Yes
B. No
Answer: B

QUESTION 132
Your company has the offices shown in the following table.
The company has an Azure Active Directory (Azure AD) tenant named contoso.com that contains a user named User1.
Users connect to a Windows Virtual Desktop deployment named WVD1. WVD1 contains session hosts that have public IP addresses from the 52.166.253.0/24 subnet.
Contoso.com has a conditional access policy that has the following settings: Name: Policy1 Assignments:
- Users and groups: User1
Cloud apps or actions: Windows Virtual Desktop Access controls:
Grant: Grant access, Require multi-factor authentication Enable policy: On
For each of the following statements, select Yes if the statement is true. Otherwise, select No. NOTE: Each correct selection is worth one point.
Hot Area:
A. Mastered
B. Not Mastered
Answer: A

QUESTION 133
Note: This question is part of a series of questions that present the same scenario. Each question in the series contains a unique solution that might meet the stated goals. Some question sets might have more than one correct solution, while others might not have a correct solution.
After you answer a question in this section, you will NOT be able to return to it. As a result, these questions will not appear in the review screen.
You have a Windows Virtual Desktop host pool named Pool1 that is integrated with an Azure Active Directory Domain Services (Azure AD DS) managed domain. You need to configure idle session timeout settings for users that connect to the session hosts in Pool1. Solution: From an Azure AD DS-joined computer, you modify the AADDC Users GPO settings.

Does that meet the goal?

C. Yes
D. No
Answer: B

QUESTION 134
Note: This question is part of a series of questions that present the same scenario. Each question in the series contains a unique solution that might meet the stated goals. Some question sets might have more than one correct solution, while others might not have a correct solution.
After you answer a question in this section, you will NOT be able to return to it. As a result, these questions will not appear in the review screen.
You have a Windows Virtual Desktop host pool named Pool1 that is integrated with an Azure Active Directory Domain Services (Azure AD DS) managed domain. You need to configure idle session timeout settings for users that connect to the session hosts in Pool1.
Solution: From the Azure portal, you modify the Session behavior settings in the RDP Properties of Pool1. Does that meet the goal?

A. Yes
B. No
Answer: B

QUESTION 135
You have a Windows Virtual Desktop deployment that contains the following:
A host pool named Pool1
Two session hosts named Host1 and Host2
An application group named RemoteAppGroup1 that contains a RemoteApp named App1 You need to prevent users from copying and pasting between App1 and their local device. What should you do?

A. Create an AppLocker policy.
B. Modify the locks of RemoteAppGroup1.
C. Modify the locks of RemoteAppGroup1.
D. Modify the RDP Properties of Pool1.
Answer: D

QUESTION 136
You have a Windows Virtual Desktop host pool named Pool1.
You are troubleshooting an issue for a Remote Desktop client that stopped responding.
You need to restore the default Remote Desktop client settings and unsubscribe from all workspaces. Which command should you run?

A. msrdcw
B. resetengine
C. mstsc
D. resetpluginhost

Answer: A

QUESTION 137

Your network contains an on-premises Active Directory domain and a Windows Virtual Desktop deployment. The computer accounts for all the session hosts are in an organizational unit (OU) named WVDHostsOU. All user accounts are in an OU named CorpUsers.

A domain administrator creates a Group Policy Object (GPO) named Policy1 that only contains user settings. The administrator links Policy1 to WVDHostsOU. You discover that when users sign in to the session hosts, none of the settings from Policy1 are applied.

What should you configure to apply GPO settings to the users when they sign in to the session hosts?

A. loopback processing
B. FSLogix profiles
C. mandatory Roaming User Profiles
D. restricted groups
Answer: A

QUESTION 138

You have a Windows Virtual Desktop deployment.

You need to provide external users with access to the deployment. The external users have computers that run Windows 10 Pro and Windows 10 Enterprise. The users do not have the ability to install applications. What should you recommend that the users use to connect to the deployment?

A. Microsoft Edge
B. RemoteApp and Desktop Connection
C. Remote Desktop Manager
D. Remote Desktop Connection
Answer: A

QUESTION 139

You network contains an on-premises Active Directory domain. The domain contains a universal security group named WVDusers. You have a hybrid Azure Active Directory (Azure AD) tenant. WVDusers syncs to Azure AD.

You have a Windows Virtual Desktop host pool that contains four Windows 10 Enterprise multi-session hosts.

You need to ensure that only the members of WVDusers can establish Windows Virtual Desktop sessions to the host pool. What should you do?

A. Assign WVDusers to an Azure role scoped to each host pool.
B. On each session host, add WVDusers to the local Remote Desktop Users group.
C. Assign WVDusers to an Azure role scoped to the session hosts.
D. Assign WVDusers to an application group.

Answer: D

QUESTION 140
You have a Windows Virtual Desktop host pool named Pool1 and an Azure Automation account named account1. Pool1 is integrated with an Azure Active Directory Domain Services (Azure AD DS) managed domain named contoso.com.
You plan to configure scaling for Pool1 by using Azure Automation runbooks.
You need to authorize the runbooks to manage the scaling of Pool1. The solution must minimize administrative effort. What should you configure?

A. a managed identity in Azure Active Directory (Azure AD)
B. a group Managed Service Account (gMSA) in Azure AD DS
C. a Connections shared resource in Azure Automation
D. a Run As account in Azure Automation
Answer: D

QUESTION 141
You have a Windows Virtual Desktop host pool named Pool1 that runs Windows 10 Enterprise multi-session hosts.
You need to use Performance Monitor to troubleshoot a low frame quality issue that is affecting a current use session to Pool1. What should you run to retrieve the user session ID?

A. Get-ComputerInfo
B. qwinsta
C. whoami
D. Get-LocalUser
Answer: B

QUESTION 142
You have an Azure subscription that contains the resources shown in the following table.

Which resources can you back up by using Azure Backup?
A. WVDVM-0 and share1 only
B. WVDVM-0 only
C. WVDVM-0, Image1, and Image2 only
D. WVDVM-0, share1, and Image1 only
E. WVDVM-0, share1, Image1, and Image2
Answer: A

QUESTION 143
DRAG DROP
You have a Windows Virtual Desktop host pool named Pool1. Pool1 contains session hosts that use FSLogix profile containers hosted in Azure NetApp Files volumes. You need to back up profile files by using snapshots.
Which three actions should you perform in sequence? To answer, move the appropriate actions from the list of actions to the answer area and arrange them in the correct order.

A. Mastered
B. Not Mastered
Answer: A

QUESTION 144
You plan to implement the FSLogix profile containers for the Seattle office. Which storage account should you use?

A. storage2
B. storage4
C. storage3
D. storage1
Answer: A

QUESTION 145
Which role should you assign to Operator2 to meet the technical requirements?

A. Desktop Virtualization Session Host Operator
B. Desktop Virtualization Host Pool Contributor
C. Desktop Virtualization User Session Operator
D. Desktop Virtualization Contributor
Answer: B

QUESTION 146
Which users can create Pool4, and which users can join session hosts to the domain? To answer, select the appropriate options in the answer area. NOTE: Each correct selection is worth one point.
A. Mastered
B. Not Mastered
Answer: A

QUESTION 147
You need to recommend an authentication solution that meets the performance requirements. Which two actions should you include in the recommendation? Each correct answer presents part of the solution. NOTE: Each correct selection is worth one point.
A. Join all the session hosts to Azure AD.
B. In each Azure region that will contain the Windows Virtual Desktop session hosts, create an Azure Active Directory Domain Service (Azure AD DS) managed domain.
C. Deploy domain controllers for the on-premises Active Directory domain on Azure virtual machines.
D. Deploy read-only domain controllers (RODCs) on Azure virtual machines.
E. In each Azure region that will contain the Windows Virtual Desktop session hosts, create an Active Directory site.
Answer: AC

QUESTION 148
DRAG DROP

You need to ensure that you can implement user profile shares for the Boston office users. The solution must meet the user profile requirements.
Which four actions should you perform in sequence? To answer, move the appropriate actions from the list of actions to the answer area and arrange them in the correct order.
A. Mastered
B. Not Mastered
Answer: A

QUESTION 149
You need to configure the device redirection settings. The solution must meet the technical requirements. Where should you configure the settings?

A. Workspace1
B. MontrealUsers
C. Group1
D. Pool1
Answer: D

QUESTION 150
You have the devices shown in the following table.
You plan to deploy Windows Virtual Desktop for client access to remove virtualized apps. Which devices support the Remote Desktop client?

A. Device1 and Device2 only
B. Device1 and Device3 only
C. Device1, Device2, and Device3
D. Device1 only
Answer: B

QUESTION 151
You plan to deploy Windows Virtual Desktop to meet the department requirements shown in the following table

You plan to use Windows Virtual Desktop host pools with load balancing and autoscaling.
You need to recommend a host pool design that meets the requirements. The solution must minimize costs. What is the minimum number of host pools you should recommend?

A. 1
B. 2
C. 3
D. 4
Answer: C

QUESTION 152
You deploy a Windows Virtual Desktop host pool named Pool1.

You have an Azure Storage account named store1 that stores FSLogix profile containers in a share named profiles. You need to configure the path to the storage containers for the session hosts. Which path should you use?

A. \\store1.blob.core.windows.net\profiles
B. https://store1.file.core.windows.net/profiles
C. \\store1.file.core.windows.net\profiles
D. https://store1.blob.core.windows.net/profiles
Answer: C

QUESTION 153
You have a Windows Virtual Desktop host pool that has a max session limit of 15. Disconnected sessions are signed out immediately. The session hosts for the host pool are shown in the following exhibit.
Use the drop-down menus to select the answer choice that completes each statement based on the information presented in the graphic. NOTE: Each correct selection is worth one point.
A. Mastered
B. Not Mastered
Answer: A

QUESTION 154
You have an Azure subscription that contains the virtual machines shown in the following table.

You create a shared image gallery as shown in the SharedGallery1 exhibit. (Click the SharedGallery1 tab.)
You create an image definition as shown in the Image1 exhibit. (Click the Image1 tab.)
For each of the following statements, select Yes if the statement is true. Otherwise, select No. NOTE: Each correct selection is worth one point.
Hot Area:
A. Mastered
B. Not Mastered
Answer: A

QUESTION 155
You have a Windows Virtual Desktop host pool named Pool1 and an Azure Storage account named Storage1. Storage1 stores FSLogix profile containers in a share folder named share1. You create a new group named Group1. You provide Group1 with permission to sign in to Pool1.
You need to ensure that the members of Group1 can store the FSLogix profile containers in share1. The solution must use the principle of least privilege. Which two privileges should you assign to Group1? Each correct answer presents part of the solution.
NOTE: Each correct selection is worth one point.

A. the Storage Blob Data Contributor role for storage1
B. the List folder / read data NTFS permissions for share1
C. the Modify NTFS permissions for share1
D. the Storage File Data SMB Share Reader role for storage1

E. the Storage File Data SMB Share Elevated Contributor role for storage1
F. the Storage File Data SMB Share Contributor role for storage1

Answer: CF

QUESTION 156
You have a Windows Virtual Desktop host pool.
You need to install Microsoft Antimalware for Azure on the session hosts. What should you do?

A. Add an extension to each session host.
B. From a Group Policy Object (GPO), enable Windows 10 security features.
C. Configure the RDP Properties of the host pool.
D. Sign in to each session host and install a Windows feature.
Answer: A

QUESTION 157
You have a Windows Virtual Desktop deployment.
You need to ensure that all the connections to the managed resources in the host pool require multi-factor authentication (MFA). Which two settings should you modify in a conditional access policy? To answer, select the appropriate options in the answer area. NOTE: Each correct selection is worth one point.
A. Mastered
B. Not Mastered
Answer: A Explanation:

QUESTION 158
Your company has the offices shown in the following table.

The company has an Azure Active Directory (Azure AD) tenant named contoso.com that contains a user named User1.
Users connect to a Windows Virtual Desktop deployment named WVD1. WVD1 contains session hosts that have public IP addresses from the 52.166.253.0/24 subnet.
Contoso.com has a conditional access policy that has the following settings: Name: Policy1 Assignments:
- Users and groups: User1
Cloud apps or actions: Windows Virtual Desktop Access controls:
Grant: Grant access, Require multi-factor authentication Enable policy: On
For each of the following statements, select Yes if the statement is true. Otherwise, select No. NOTE: Each correct selection is worth one point.
Hot Area:
A. Mastered
B. Not Mastered
Answer: A

QUESTION 159

Note: This question is part of a series of questions that present the same scenario. Each question in the series contains a unique solution that might meet the stated goals. Some question sets might have more than one correct solution, while others might not have a correct solution.
After you answer a question in this section, you will NOT be able to return to it. As a result, these questions will not appear in the review screen.
You have a Windows Virtual Desktop host pool named Pool1 that is integrated with an Azure Active Directory Domain Services (Azure AD DS) managed domain. You need to configure idle session timeout settings for users that connect to the session hosts in Pool1.
Solution: From an Azure AD DS-joined computer, you modify the AADDC Computers GPO settings. Does that meet the goal?

A. Yes
B. No
Answer: A

QUESTION 156
Note: This question is part of a series of questions that present the same scenario. Each question in the series contains a unique solution that might meet the stated goals. Some question sets might have more than one correct solution, while others might not have a correct solution.
After you answer a question in this section, you will NOT be able to return to it. As a result, these questions will not appear in the review screen.
You have a Windows Virtual Desktop host pool named Pool1 that is integrated with an Azure Active Directory Domain Services (Azure AD DS) managed domain. You need to configure idle session timeout settings for users that connect to the session hosts in Pool1.
Solution: From the Azure portal, you modify the Session behavior settings in the RDP Properties of Pool1. Does that meet the goal?

A. Yes
B. No
Answer: B

QUESTION 157
You have a Windows Virtual Desktop deployment. You publish a RemoteApp named AppVersion1.
You need AppVersion1 to appear in the Remote Desktop client as Sales Contact Application. Which PowerShell cmdlet should you use?

A. New-AzADApplication
B. Update-AzWvdApplicationGroup
C. Register-AzWvdApplicationGroup
D. Update-AzWvdApplication
Answer: D

QUESTION 158
You have a Windows Virtual Desktop deployment that contains the following:
A host pool named Pool1

Two session hosts named Host1 and Host2
An application group named RemoteAppGroup1 that contains a RemoteApp named App1 You need to prevent users from copying and pasting between App1 and their local device. What should you do?

A. Create an AppLocker policy.
B. Modify the locks of RemoteAppGroup1.
C. Modify the locks of RemoteAppGroup1.
D. Modify the RDP Properties of Pool1.
Answer: D

QUESTION 159
You network contains an on-premises Active Directory domain that syncs to an Azure Active Directory (Azure AD) tenant. The domain contains the users shown in the following table.
You have a Windows Virtual Desktop deployment that contains the application groups shown in the following table. You have the workspaces shown in the following table.
For each of the following statements, select Yes if the statement is true. Otherwise, select No. NOTE: Each correct selection is worth one point.
A. Mastered
B. Not Mastered
Answer: A

QUESTION 160
You have a Windows Virtual Desktop host pool that contains two session hosts. The Microsoft Teams client is installed on each session host.
You discover that only the Microsoft Teams chat and collaboration features work. The calling and meeting features are disabled. You need to ensure that users can set the calling and meeting features from within Microsoft Teams.
What should you do?

A. Install the Remote Desktop WebRTC Redirector Service.
B. Configure Remote audio mode in the RDP Properties.
C. Install the Teams Meeting add-in for Outlook.
D. Configure audio input redirection.

Answer: A

QUESTION 161
You have a Windows Virtual Desktop host pool that contains 20 Windows 10 Enterprise multi-session hosts.
Users connect to the Windows Virtual Desktop deployment from computers that run Windows 10. You plan to implement FSLogix Application Masking. You need to deploy Application Masking rule sets. The solution must minimize administrative effort. To where should you copy the rule sets?

A. the FSLogix profile container of each user

B. C:\Program Files\FSLogix\Apps\Rules on every Windows 10 computer
C. C:\Program Files\FSLogix\Apps\Rules on every session host
Answer: C

QUESTION 162
You network contains an on-premises Active Directory domain. The domain contains a universal security group named WVDusers. You have a hybrid Azure Active Directory (Azure AD) tenant. WVDusers syncs to Azure AD.
You have a Windows Virtual Desktop host pool that contains four Windows 10 Enterprise multi-session hosts.
You need to ensure that only the members of WVDusers can establish Windows Virtual Desktop sessions to the host pool. What should you do?

A. Assign WVDusers to an Azure role scoped to each host pool.
B. On each session host, add WVDusers to the local Remote Desktop Users group.
C. Assign WVDusers to an Azure role scoped to the session hosts.
D. Assign WVDusers to an application group.
Answer: D

QUESTION 163
You have an Azure subscription that contains the resources shown in the following table.
Which resources can you back up by using Azure Backup?

A. WVDVM-0 and share1 only
B. WVDVM-0 only
C. WVDVM-0, Image1, and Image2 only
D. WVDVM-0, share1, and Image1 only
E. WVDVM-0, share1, Image1, and Image2
Answer: A

QUESTION 164
You are planning the deployment of Pool4.
What will be the maximum number of users that can connect to Pool4, and how many session hosts are needed to support five concurrent user sessions? To answer, select the appropriate options in the answer area.
NOTE: Each correct selection is worth one point.
A. Mastered
B. Not Mastered
Answer: A

QUESTION 165
You plan to implement the FSLogix profile containers for the Seattle office. Which storage account should you use?

A. storage2
B. storage4

C. storage3
D. storage1
Answer: A

QUESTION 166
Which role should you assign to Operator2 to meet the technical requirements?
A. Desktop Virtualization Session Host Operator
B. Desktop Virtualization Host Pool Contributor
C. Desktop Virtualization User Session Operator
D. Desktop Virtualization Contributor
Answer: B

QUESTION 167
You need to recommend an authentication solution that meets the performance requirements. Which two actions should you include in the recommendation? Each correct answer presents part of the solution. NOTE: Each correct selection is worth one point.

A. Join all the session hosts to Azure AD.
B. In each Azure region that will contain the Windows Virtual Desktop session hosts, create an Azure Active Directory Domain Service (Azure AD DS) managed domain.
C. Deploy domain controllers for the on-premises Active Directory domain on Azure virtual machines.
D. Deploy read-only domain controllers (RODCs) on Azure virtual machines.
E. In each Azure region that will contain the Windows Virtual Desktop session hosts, create an Active Directory site.
Answer: AC

QUESTION 168
DRAG DROP
You need to ensure that you can implement user profile shares for the Boston office users. The solution must meet the user profile requirements.
Which four actions should you perform in sequence? To answer, move the appropriate actions from the list of actions to the answer area and arrange them in the correct order.
A. Mastered
B. Not Mastered
Answer: A

QUESTION 169
Which two roles should you assign to Admin1 to meet the security requirements? Each correct answer presents part of the solution. NOTE: Each correct selection is worth one point.

A. Desktop Virtualization Host Pool Contributor
B. Desktop Virtualization Application Group Contributor
C. Desktop Virtualization Workspace Contributor
D. Desktop Virtualization Application Group Reader
E. User Access Administrator

Answer: BC

QUESTION 170
You need to configure the device redirection settings. The solution must meet the technical requirements. Where should you configure the settings?

A. Workspace1
B. MontrealUsers
C. Group1
D. Pool1
Answer: D

QUESTION 171
You need to configure the virtual machines that have the Pool1 prefix. The solution must meet the technical requirements. What should you use?

A. a Windows Virtual Desktop automation task
B. Virtual machine auto-shutdown
C. Service Health in Azure Monitor
D. Azure Automation
Answer: A

QUESTION 172
You have the devices shown in the following table.

Name	Operating System
Device1	Windows 10 Home
Device2	Windows 8.1 Professional
Device3	Windows 10 IOT Enterprise

You plan to deploy Windows Virtual Desktop for client access to remove virtualized apps. Which devices support the Remote Desktop client?

A. Device1 and Device2 only
B. Device1 and Device3 only
C. Device1, Device2, and Device3
D. Device1 only
Answer: B

QUESTION 173
You plan to deploy Windows Virtual Desktop. The deployment will use existing virtual machines. You create a Windows Virtual Desktop host pool.
You need to ensure that you can add the virtual machines to the host pool. What should you do first?

A. Register the Microsoft.DesktopVirtualization provider.
B. Generate a registration key.
C. Run the Invoke-AzVMRunCommand cmdlet.
D. Create a role assignment.
Answer: A

QUESTION 174
You plan to deploy Windows Virtual Desktop session host virtual machines based on a preconfigured master image. The master image will be stored in a shared image. You create a virtual machine named Image1 to use as the master image. You install applications and apply configuration changes to Image1.
You need to ensure that the new session host virtual machines created based on Image1 have unique names and security identifiers. What should you do on Image1 before you add the image to the shared image gallery?

A. At a command prompt, run the set computername command.
B. At a command prompt, run the sysprep command.
C. From PowerShell, run the rename-computer cmdlet.
D. From the lock screen of the Windows device, perform a Windows Autopilot Reset.
Answer: B

QUESTION 175
Note: This question is part of a series of questions that present the same scenario. Each question in the series contains a unique solution that might meet the stated goals. Some question sets might have more than one correct solution, while others might not have a correct solution.
After you answer a question in this section, you will NOT be able to return to it. As a result, these questions will not appear in the review screen. You have a Windows Virtual Desktop host pool that contains five session hosts. The session hosts run Windows 10 Enterprise multi-session.
You need to prevent users from accessing the internet from Windows Virtual Desktop sessions. The session hosts must be allowed to access all the required Microsoft services. Solution: You configure the Address space settings of the virtual network that contains the session hosts.
Does that meet the goal?

A. Yes
B. No
Answer: B

QUESTION 176
Note: This question is part of a series of questions that present the same scenario. Each question in the series contains a unique solution that might meet the stated goals. Some question sets might have more than one correct solution, while others might not have a correct solution.
After you answer a question in this section, you will NOT be able to return to it. As a result, these questions will not appear in the review screen. You have a Windows Virtual Desktop host pool that contains five session hosts. The session hosts run Windows 10 Enterprise multi-session.
You need to prevent users from accessing the internet from Windows Virtual Desktop sessions. The session hosts must be allowed to access all the required Microsoft services.

Solution: You modify the IP configuration of each session host. Does that meet the goal?

A. Yes
B. No
Answer: B

QUESTION 177
You have a Windows Virtual Desktop host pool named Pool1 and an Azure Storage account named Storage1. Storage1 stores FSLogix profile containers in a share folder named share1. You create a new group named Group1. You provide Group1 with permission to sign in to Pool1.
You need to ensure that the members of Group1 can store the FSLogix profile containers in share1. The solution must use the principle of least privilege. Which two privileges should you assign to Group1? Each correct answer presents part of the solution.
NOTE: Each correct selection is worth one point.

A. the Storage Blob Data Contributor role for storage1
B. the List folder / read data NTFS permissions for share1
C. the Modify NTFS permissions for share1
D. the Storage File Data SMB Share Reader role for storage1
E. the Storage File Data SMB Share Elevated Contributor role for storage1
F. the Storage File Data SMB Share Contributor role for storage1
Answer: CF

QUESTION 178

Your company has the offices shown in the following table.

Location	Internet network IP address space	Public IP address space
Boston	10.10.0.0/16	13.83.131.0/24
Seattle	172.16.0.0/16	92.15.10.0/24

The company has an Azure Active Directory (Azure AD) tenant named contoso.com that contains a user named User1.
Users connect to a Windows Virtual Desktop deployment named WVD1. WVD1 contains session hosts that have public IP addresses from the 52.166.253.0/24 subnet.
Contoso.com has a conditional access policy that has the following settings:
Name: Policy1 Assignments:
- Users and groups: User1
- Cloud apps or actions: Windows Virtual Desktop Access controls:
- Grant: Grant access, Require multi-factor authentication Enable policy: On

For each of the following statements, select Yes if the statement is true. Otherwise, select No.
NOTE: Each correct selection is worth one point. Hot Area:

Statements	Yes/No
If User1 connects to Windows Virtual Desktop from the office in Boston, User1 is prompted for multi-factor authentication (MFA).	Yes
If User1 connects to Windows Virtual Desktop from home, User1 is prompted for multi-factor authentication (MFA).	Yes
If User1 connects to Microsoft Exchange Online from a Windows Virtual Desktop session, User1 is prompted for multi-factor authentication (MFA).	Yes

A. Mastered
B. Not Mastered
Answer: A

QUESTION 179
Note: This question is part of a series of questions that present the same scenario. Each question in the series contains a unique solution that might meet the stated goals. Some question sets might have more than one correct solution, while others might not have a correct solution.
After you answer a question in this section, you will NOT be able to return to it. As a result, these questions will not appear in the review screen.
You have a Windows Virtual Desktop host pool named Pool1 that is integrated with an Azure Active Directory Domain Services (Azure AD DS) managed domain. You need to configure idle session timeout settings for users that connect to the session hosts in Pool1. Solution: From an Azure AD DS-joined computer, you modify the AADDC Users GPO settings.
Does that meet the goal?

A. Yes
B. No
Answer: B

QUESTION 180
Note: This question is part of a series of questions that present the same scenario. Each question in the series contains a unique solution that might meet the stated goals. Some question sets might have more than one correct solution, while others might not have a correct solution.
After you answer a question in this section, you will NOT be able to return to it. As a result, these questions will not appear in the review screen.
You have a Windows Virtual Desktop host pool named Pool1 that is integrated with an Azure Active Directory Domain Services (Azure AD DS) managed domain.
You need to configure idle session timeout settings for users that connect to the session hosts in Pool1. Solution: From an Azure AD DS-joined computer, you modify the AADDC Computers GPO settings.
Does that meet the goal?

A. Yes

B. No
Answer: A

QUESTION 181
Note: This question is part of a series of questions that present the same scenario. Each question in the series contains a unique solution that might meet the stated goals. Some question sets might have more than one correct solution, while others might not have a correct solution.
After you answer a question in this section, you will NOT be able to return to it. As a result, these questions will not appear in the review screen.
You have a Windows Virtual Desktop host pool named Pool1 that is integrated with an Azure Active Directory Domain Services (Azure AD DS) managed domain. You need to configure idle session timeout settings for users that connect to the session hosts in Pool1.
Solution: From the Azure portal, you modify the Session behavior settings in the RDP Properties of Pool1. Does that meet the goal?

A. Yes
B. No
Answer: B

QUESTION 182
You have a Windows Virtual Desktop deployment. You publish a RemoteApp named AppVersion1.
You need AppVersion1 to appear in the Remote Desktop client as Sales Contact Application. Which PowerShell cmdlet should you use?
A. New-AzADApplication
B. Update-AzWvdApplicationGroup
C. Register-AzWvdApplicationGroup
D. Update-AzWvdApplication
Answer: D

QUESTION 183
Your network contains an on-premises Active Directory domain and a Windows Virtual Desktop deployment. The computer accounts for all the session hosts are in an organizational unit (OU) named WVDHostsOU. All user accounts are in an OU named CorpUsers.
A domain administrator creates a Group Policy Object (GPO) named Policy1 that only contains user settings. The administrator links Policy1 to WVDHostsOU. You discover that when users sign in to the session hosts, none of the settings from Policy1 are applied.
What should you configure to apply GPO settings to the users when they sign in to the session hosts?
A. loopback processing
B. FSLogix profiles
C. mandatory Roaming User Profiles
D. restricted groups
Answer: A

QUESTION 184

You network contains an on-premises Active Directory domain. The domain contains a universal security group named WVDusers. You have a hybrid Azure Active Directory (Azure AD) tenant. WVDusers syncs to Azure AD.
You have a Windows Virtual Desktop host pool that contains four Windows 10 Enterprise multi-session hosts.
You need to ensure that only the members of WVDusers can establish Windows Virtual Desktop sessions to the host pool. What should you do?

A. Assign WVDusers to an Azure role scoped to each host pool.
B. On each session host, add WVDusers to the local Remote Desktop Users group.
C. Assign WVDusers to an Azure role scoped to the session hosts.
D. Assign WVDusers to an application group.
Answer: D

QUESTION 185
You have a Windows Virtual Desktop host pool named Pool1 that runs Windows 10 Enterprise multi-session hosts.
You need to use Performance Monitor to troubleshoot a low frame quality issue that is affecting a current use session to Pool1. What should you run to retrieve the user session ID?
A. Get-ComputerInfo
B. qwinsta
C. whoami
D. Get-LocalUser
Answer: B
QUESTION 186
You have an Azure subscription that contains the resources shown in the following table.

Name	Description
WVDVM-0	A virtual machine used in a pooled virtual machine set
Share1	An Azure file share that stores FSLogix profile containers
Image1	A custom Windows 10 image in a shared image gallery
Image2	A custom Windows Server 2019 image stored in Azure Blob storage

Which resources can you back up by using Azure Backup?
A. WVDVM-0 and share1 only
B. WVDVM-0 only
C. WVDVM-0, Image1, and Image2 only
D. WVDVM-0, share1, and Image1 only
E. WVDVM-0, share1, Image1, and Image2
Answer: A

QUESTION 187
DRAG DROP

You need to evaluate the RDS deployment in the Seattle office. The solution must meet the technical requirements.

Which three actions should you perform in sequence? To answer, move the appropriate actions from the list of actions to the answer area and arrange them in the correct order.

Actions	Answer Area
Create a project in Azure Migrate.	
Register the Lakeside tool with Azure Migrate	
Add the Azure Advisor recommendation digest	
Install agents on the virtual machines that have the Pool3 prefix.	
Install agents on the virtual machines that have the Pool2 prefix.	
Create a Recovery Service vault.	

A. Mastered

B. Not Mastered

Answer: A

QUESTION 188

Which users can create Pool4, and which users can join session hosts to the domain? To answer, select the appropriate options in the answer area. NOTE: Each correct selection is worth one point.

Answer area
Can Create Pool4: 1. Admin2 only 2. Admin2 and Admin4 only 3. Admin1, Admin2 and Admin4 only 4. Admin2, Admin3, and Admin4 only 5. Admin1, Admin2, Admin3, and Admin4
Can join session hosts to the domain: 1 Operator only 2. Admin1 and Admin3 only 3. Operator1 and Admin1 only 4. Operator1 and Operator3 only 5. Operator1, Operator2, Operator3

A. Mastered

B. Not Mastered

Answer: A

QUESTION 189

DRAG DROP

You need to ensure that you can implement user profile shares for the Boston office users. The solution must meet the user profile requirements.

Which four actions should you perform in sequence? To answer, move the appropriate actions from the list of actions to the answer area and arrange them in the correct order.

Actions	Answer Area
Create a file share and configure share permissions.	
Sign in to VM1 as Admin1.	
Run the Join-AzStorageAccountForAuthCmdlet.	
Sign in to VM1 as CloudAdmin1.	
Install the AzFilesHybrid PowerShell module.	

A. Mastered
B. Not Mastered
Answer: A

QUESTION 190
You need to configure the user settings of Admin1 to meet the user profile requirements. What should you do?

A. Modify the membership of the FSLogix ODFC Exclude List group.
B. Modify the membership of the FSLogix Profile Exclude List group.
C. Modify the HKLM\SOFTWARE\FSLogix\Profiles registry settings.
D. Modify the HKLM\SOFTWARE\FSLogix\ODFC registry settings.
Answer: A

QUESTION 191
You have the devices shown in the following table.
You plan to deploy Windows Virtual Desktop for client access to remove virtualized apps. Which devices support the Remote Desktop client?

A. Device1 and Device2 only
B. Device1 and Device3 only
C. Device1, Device2, and Device3
D. Device1 only
Answer: B

QUESTION 192
You have a Windows Virtual Desktop host pool that has a max session limit of 15. Disconnected sessions are signed out immediately. The session hosts for the host pool are shown in the following exhibit.

Use the drop-down menus to select the answer choice that completes each statement based on the information presented in the graphic. NOTE: Each correct selection is worth one point.
A. Mastered
B. Not Mastered

Answer: A

QUESTION 193

You have an Azure virtual machine named VM1 that runs Windows 10 Enterprise multi-session. You plan to add language packs to VM1 and create a custom image of VM1 for a Windows Virtual Desktop host pool.
You need to ensure that modern apps can use the additional language packs when you deploy session hosts by using the custom image. Which command should you run first? To answer, select the appropriate options in the answer area.
NOTE: Each correct selection is worth one point. Hot Area:
A. Mastered
B. Not Mastered
Answer: A

QUESTION 194
You have a shared image gallery that contains the Windows 10 images shown in the following table.
You create a Windows Virtual Desktop deployment that has the following settings:
Host pool name: Pool1 Location: West US
Host pool type: Personal
Which images can you use for the session hosts?

A. Image1 only
B. Image1, Image2, Image3, and Image4
C. Image2 only
D. Image1 and Image2 only
E. Image1 and Image3 only
Answer: E

QUESTION 195
DRAG DROP
You plan to deploy Windows Virtual Desktop.
You need to create Azure NetApp Files storage to store FSLogix profile containers.
Which four actions should you perform in sequence after you register the NetApp Resource Provider? To answer, move the appropriate actions from the list of actions to the answer area and arrange them in the correct order.
NOTE: More than one order of answer choices is correct. You will receive credit for any of the correct orders you select.
A. Mastered
B. Not Mastered
Answer: A

QUESTION 196

Note: This question is part of a series of questions that present the same scenario. Each question in the series contains a unique solution that might meet the stated goals. Some question sets might have more than one correct solution, while others might not have a correct solution.
After you answer a question in this section, you will NOT be able to return to it. As a result, these questions will not appear in the review screen. You have a Windows Virtual Desktop host pool that contains five session hosts. The session hosts run Windows 10 Enterprise multi-session.
You need to prevent users from accessing the internet from Windows Virtual Desktop sessions. The session hosts must be allowed to access all the required Microsoft services. Solution: You configure rules in the network security group (NSG) linked to the subnet of the session hosts.
Does that meet the goal?

A. Yes
B. No
Answer: A

QUESTION 197
Note: This question is part of a series of questions that present the same scenario. Each question in the series contains a unique solution that might meet the stated goals. Some question sets might have more than one correct solution, while others might not have a correct solution.
After you answer a question in this section, you will NOT be able to return to it. As a result, these questions will not appear in the review screen. You have a Windows Virtual Desktop host pool that contains five session hosts. The session hosts run Windows 10 Enterprise multi-session.
You need to prevent users from accessing the internet from Windows Virtual Desktop sessions. The session hosts must be allowed to access all the required Microsoft services. Solution: You configure the Address space settings of the virtual network that contains the session hosts.
Does that meet the goal?

A. Yes
B. No
Answer: B

QUESTION 198
Your company has the offices shown in the following table.
The company has an Azure Active Directory (Azure AD) tenant named contoso.com that contains a user named User1.
Users connect to a Windows Virtual Desktop deployment named WVD1. WVD1 contains session hosts that have public IP addresses from the 52.166.253.0/24 subnet.
Contoso.com has a conditional access policy that has the following settings: Name: Policy1 Assignments:
- Users and groups: User1
Cloud apps or actions: Windows Virtual Desktop Access controls:
Grant: Grant access, Require multi-factor authentication Enable policy: On
For each of the following statements, select Yes if the statement is true. Otherwise, select No.
NOTE: Each correct selection is worth one point.
Hot Area:
A. Mastered

B. Not Mastered
Answer: A

QUESTION 199
Note: This question is part of a series of questions that present the same scenario. Each question in the series contains a unique solution that might meet the stated goals. Some question sets might have more than one correct solution, while others might not have a correct solution.
After you answer a question in this section, you will NOT be able to return to it. As a result, these questions will not appear in the review screen.
You have a Windows Virtual Desktop host pool named Pool1 that is integrated with an Azure Active Directory Domain Services (Azure AD DS) managed domain. You need to configure idle session timeout settings for users that connect to the session hosts in Pool1. Solution: From an Azure AD DS-joined computer, you modify the AADDC Users GPO settings.
Does that meet the goal?

A. Yes
B. No
Answer: B

QUESTION 200
Note: This question is part of a series of questions that present the same scenario. Each question in the series contains a unique solution that might meet the stated goals. Some question sets might have more than one correct solution, while others might not have a correct solution.
After you answer a question in this section, you will NOT be able to return to it. As a result, these questions will not appear in the review screen.
You have a Windows Virtual Desktop host pool named Pool1 that is integrated with an Azure Active Directory Domain Services (Azure AD DS) managed domain. You need to configure idle session timeout settings for users that connect to the session hosts in Pool1.
Solution: From the Azure portal, you modify the Session behavior settings in the RDP Properties of Pool1. Does that meet the goal?

A. Yes
B. No
Answer: B

QUESTION 201
You have a Windows Virtual Desktop deployment that contains the following:
A host pool named Pool1
Two session hosts named Host1 and Host2
An application group named RemoteAppGroup1 that contains a RemoteApp named App1 You need to prevent users from copying and pasting between App1 and their local device. What should you do?

A. Create an AppLocker policy.
B. Modify the locks of RemoteAppGroup1.
C. Modify the locks of RemoteAppGroup1.

D. Modify the RDP Properties of Pool1.
Answer: D

QUESTION 202
You have a Windows Virtual Desktop host pool named Pool1.
You are troubleshooting an issue for a Remote Desktop client that stopped responding.
You need to restore the default Remote Desktop client settings and unsubscribe from all workspaces. Which command should you run?

A. msrdcw
B. resetengine
C. mstsc
D. resetpluginhost
Answer: A

QUESTION 203
Your network contains an on-premises Active Directory domain and a Windows Virtual Desktop deployment. The computer accounts for all the session hosts are in an organizational unit (OU) named WVDHostsOU. All user accounts are in an OU named CorpUsers.
A domain administrator creates a Group Policy Object (GPO) named Policy1 that only contains user settings. The administrator links Policy1 to WVDHostsOU. You discover that when users sign in to the session hosts, none of the settings from Policy1 are applied.
What should you configure to apply GPO settings to the users when they sign in to the session hosts?

A. loopback processing
B. FSLogix profiles
C. mandatory Roaming User Profiles
D. restricted groups
Answer: A

QUESTION 204
You have a Windows Virtual Desktop deployment.
You need to provide external users with access to the deployment. The external users have computers that run Windows 10 Pro and Windows 10 Enterprise. The users do not have the ability to install applications. What should you recommend that the users use to connect to the deployment?

A. Microsoft Edge
B. RemoteApp and Desktop Connection
C. Remote Desktop Manager
D. Remote Desktop Connection
Answer: A

ONLINE RESOURCES

Practice Paper

Link : https://forms.gle/on5iJVnuPGeKaEqs8

QR Code :

Video Content

Link :
https://www.youtube.com/playlist?list=PLzlh_31VWEFowmPK_ro41wiljGoGKexGI

QR Code :

Chapter 3: Viva Voce Questions

Q 1: What is Azure Virtual Desktop?
Answer: Azure Virtual Desktop (AVD) is a cloud-based desktop and app virtualization service that allows users to access virtual desktops and applications from anywhere.
Q 2: How does AVD support remote work?
Answer: AVD provides a secure, scalable, and flexible environment that allows users to access their desktops and applications remotely, supporting a distributed workforce.
Q 3: What are the components of Azure Virtual Desktop architecture?
Answer: The main components include Azure Virtual Machines, Azure Active Directory, and Azure Networking, integrated to deliver a seamless virtual desktop experience.
Q 4: What role does Azure Active Directory play in AVD?
Answer: Azure Active Directory provides identity services and manages user authentication and security for Azure Virtual Desktop.
Q 5: How does FSLogix enhance the user experience in AVD?
Answer: FSLogix optimizes profile loading times and provides better data management to ensure a smooth and consistent user experience across sessions.
Q 6: What is the purpose of Azure Blob Storage in AVD?
Answer: Azure Blob Storage is used to store user profiles and data, leveraging FSLogix technology to containerize and dynamically attach profiles to user sessions.
Q 7: Describe the process of scaling Azure Virtual Desktop environments.
Answer: Scaling involves adjusting the number of VMs based on user demand to optimize performance and cost, using Azure's autoscale functionality.
Q 8: How do you ensure security in Azure Virtual Desktop setups?
Answer: Security in AVD is managed through multi-factor authentication, conditional access policies, role-based access control, and data encryption.
Q 9: What is a host pool in AVD?
Answer: A host pool is a collection of Azure virtual machines that serve as host resources for users connecting to Azure Virtual Desktop.
Q 10: How does network connectivity affect AVD performance?
Answer: Network performance is crucial as it impacts the speed and responsiveness of the virtual desktops, influencing overall user experience.
Q 11: Can you migrate existing virtual desktops to AVD?
Answer: Yes, existing desktops and apps can be migrated to AVD, leveraging Azure's migration tools and services for a seamless transition.
Q 12: What are application groups in AVD?
Answer: Application groups are used to manage and assign applications to users within Azure Virtual Desktop environments.
Q 13: Explain the cost management strategies for AVD.
Answer: Cost management includes selecting appropriate VM sizes, using reserved instances, and scaling resources based on demand to optimize expenditures.
Q 14: What monitoring tools are available for AVD?
Answer: Azure Monitor and Azure Insights provide tools to track performance, usage, and operational health of Azure Virtual Desktop deployments.
Q 15: How do you troubleshoot issues in AVD?

Answer: Troubleshooting involves analyzing diagnostic logs, monitoring performance metrics, and using Azure's troubleshooting and support tools.

Q 16: What is the benefit of session host load balancing in AVD?

Answer: Session host load balancing ensures that user sessions are evenly distributed across available hosts, enhancing performance and reliability.

Q 17: How do you manage updates in an AVD environment?

Answer: Updates are managed through automation tools like Azure Update Management, ensuring that VMs are regularly updated without user disruption.

Q 18: What licensing is required for Azure Virtual Desktop?

Answer: AVD requires appropriate Microsoft 365 or Windows 10/11 enterprise licenses, which include access to Azure Virtual Desktop.

Q 19: Can AVD be integrated with on-premises environments?

Answer: Yes, AVD can be integrated with on-premises networks through Azure VPN or ExpressRoute, providing a hybrid cloud setup.

Q 20: Describe the user profile management in AVD.

Answer: User profiles in AVD are managed through FSLogix, which provides dynamic attachment of user profiles stored in Azure Blob Storage during sessions.

YouTube Link for Viva Voce Questions:
https://www.youtube.com/playlist?list=PLzlh_31VWEFrYJh2O637Xhv7PhA9pCezM

QR Code:

YouTube Videos Playlists for all Microsoft Certifications Videos

Microsoft Azure AI Fundamentals AZ-900
Link: https://www.youtube.com/playlist?list=PLzlh_31VWEFq9KU8Gr0ISbfj-TW6k17f8

QR Code:

Microsoft Azure Administrator AZ-104 Microsoft Azure Virtual Desktop AZ-140
Link: https://www.youtube.com/playlist?list=PLzlh_31VWEFq7JHJMuPJZcw-XShaPrUYP

QR Code:

Microsoft Azure Virtual Desktop AZ-140
Link: https://www.youtube.com/playlist?list=PLzlh_31VWEFowmPK_ro41wiljGoGKexGI

QR Code:

Microsoft Azure Developer AZ-204
Link:
https://www.youtube.com/playlist?list=PLzlh_31VWEFqT72UPVCUi6rqRqLBuwMSr

QR Code:

Designing Microsoft Azure Infrastructure Solution AZ-305
Link:
https://www.youtube.com/playlist?list=PLzlh_31VWEFpTerOknh9kgL4eTbhQwDND

QR Code:

Microsoft Azure Devops Engineer AZ-400
Link: https://www.youtube.com/playlist?list=PLzlh_31VWEFpyUIe_DuaeIkcThEfMT_BT

QR Code:

Microsoft Azure Security Engineer AZ-500
Link:
https://www.youtube.com/playlist?list=PLzlh_31VWEFqFBJgQTPNucIO0wVJdjNmS

QR Code:

Microsoft Azure Network Engineer AZ-700
Link:
https://www.youtube.com/playlist?list=PLzlh_31VWEFowujgDl16YDCvsQtmKgEqL

QR Code:

Microsoft Azure Fundamentals AZ-900
Link: https://www.youtube.com/playlist?list=PLzlh_31VWEFpeXZ2p32R1zDsgcbV8kI1K

QR Code:

Microsoft Azure Data Engineer DP-203
Link: https://www.youtube.com/playlist?list=PLzlh_31VWEFp3XTNqoS60UAOzl8NVG-5z

QR Code:

Microsoft Azure Database Administrator DP- 300
Link: https://www.youtube.com/playlist?list=PLzlh_31VWEFpv-rmc2mbpoIqUOqVW_cIo

QR Code:

AZ-140 practice questions

Q1. You need to design an Azure Virtual Desktop deployment for 300 users who require pooled desktops. Which host pool type should you choose?
A. Personal host pool
B. Pooled host pool
C. RemoteApp only host pool
D. Dedicated host pool

Answer: B. Pooled host pool
Reasoning: A pooled host pool allows multiple users to share session hosts, which is ideal when users do not need a dedicated VM. It reduces cost because session hosts are shared and can be scaled based on demand. Personal host pools assign one VM to one user, which is more suitable for users requiring persistent, dedicated desktops. RemoteApp is used when only applications are published instead of full desktops. For 300 general users, pooled desktops provide better cost efficiency, easier management, and scalable capacity.

Q2. Which component stores user profiles in Azure Virtual Desktop to provide a consistent experience across session hosts?
A. Azure Files
B. FSLogix profile containers
C. Azure Bastion
D. Azure Monitor

Answer: B. FSLogix profile containers
Reasoning: FSLogix profile containers store user profiles in a virtual hard disk file, usually on Azure Files or Azure NetApp Files. When a user signs in to any session host, the profile container attaches, giving the user a consistent desktop, settings, and application data. Azure Files may store the container, but FSLogix is the profile management technology. Azure Bastion is for secure VM access, and Azure Monitor is for monitoring. FSLogix is highly important in multi-session AVD environments.

Q3. You want to reduce latency for Azure Virtual Desktop users. What should you check first?
A. The number of application groups
B. Network round-trip time to Azure region
C. Number of assigned users
D. Desktop icon size

Answer: B. Network round-trip time to Azure region
Reasoning: User experience in Azure Virtual Desktop depends heavily on network latency between the user endpoint and the Azure region hosting session hosts. A lower round-trip time improves responsiveness. Choosing the correct Azure region close to users is one of the first design decisions. Application groups and assigned users affect management but do not directly determine latency. Desktop icon size is unrelated. For performance planning, network capacity, bandwidth, and round-trip latency must be assessed early.

Q4. Which Azure service is commonly used to monitor Azure Virtual Desktop performance and connection health?

A. Azure Monitor
B. Azure DNS
C. Azure Firewall
D. Azure Key Vault

Answer: A. Azure Monitor
Reasoning: Azure Monitor collects logs and metrics from Azure Virtual Desktop resources. It helps administrators analyze connection failures, session host performance, user sessions, errors, and capacity. Azure Virtual Desktop Insights is built on Azure Monitor Workbooks and Log Analytics. Azure DNS handles name resolution, Azure Firewall controls network traffic, and Azure Key Vault stores secrets and keys. For monitoring and troubleshooting AVD infrastructure, Azure Monitor is the primary service.

Q5. Which tool helps automatically start and stop session hosts based on usage demand?
A. Autoscale
B. Azure Policy
C. Azure Advisor only
D. Microsoft Entra Connect

Answer: A. Autoscale
Reasoning: Autoscale in Azure Virtual Desktop helps manage session host capacity by starting and stopping virtual machines based on schedules, user demand, and scaling plans. It reduces cost by shutting down unused hosts and improves availability by starting hosts when needed. Azure Policy enforces compliance rules, Azure Advisor gives recommendations, and Microsoft Entra Connect synchronizes identities. For cost optimization and session host capacity management, Autoscale is the correct feature.

Q6. You need users to access only published applications, not a full desktop. What should you configure?
A. Desktop application group
B. RemoteApp application group
C. Personal desktop assignment
D. Azure Bastion

Answer: B. RemoteApp application group
Reasoning: RemoteApp application groups publish individual applications to users instead of a complete desktop. This is useful when users need access to specific business apps while keeping the experience simple and secure. A desktop application group publishes a full desktop. Personal desktop assignment gives users dedicated desktops. Azure Bastion provides secure browser-based administrative access to VMs and is unrelated to app publishing.

Q7. Which identity option allows Azure Virtual Desktop session hosts to join Microsoft Entra ID directly without traditional Active Directory domain join?
A. Microsoft Entra join
B. Workgroup join
C. Azure Bastion join
D. Storage account join

Answer: A. Microsoft Entra join

Reasoning: Microsoft Entra joined session hosts allow organizations to deploy AVD without requiring traditional AD DS domain join. This is useful for cloud-native environments. Users authenticate through Microsoft Entra ID, and access can be controlled using Conditional Access and Azure RBAC. Workgroup join is not a recommended enterprise identity model for AVD. Azure Bastion and storage accounts are unrelated to identity join type.

Q8. What is the purpose of application groups in Azure Virtual Desktop?
A. To store FSLogix profiles
B. To group published desktops or apps for user assignment
C. To configure Azure Firewall rules
D. To create storage accounts

Answer: B. To group published desktops or apps for user assignment
Reasoning: Application groups define what users can access in Azure Virtual Desktop. They can contain a full desktop or RemoteApps. Users or groups are assigned to application groups so they can see the resources in their Remote Desktop client. FSLogix profiles are stored separately, firewall rules are configured in networking services, and storage accounts store data. Application groups are central to publishing and access assignment in AVD.

Q9. Which feature should you use to control whether clipboard, printer, or drive redirection is allowed in AVD sessions?
A. RDP properties
B. Azure Cost Management
C. Azure Backup
D. DNS private zones

Answer: A. RDP properties
Reasoning: RDP properties on a host pool control user experience settings such as clipboard redirection, printer redirection, drive redirection, audio settings, and display behavior. These settings help administrators balance usability and security. Azure Cost Management tracks spending, Azure Backup protects data, and DNS private zones handle name resolution. For device redirection control in Azure Virtual Desktop, RDP properties are the correct configuration area.

Q10. You need to securely access a session host VM for administration without exposing RDP to the internet. Which service is recommended?
A. Azure Bastion
B. Public IP address
C. Open port 3389 to all users
D. RemoteApp

Answer: A. Azure Bastion
Reasoning: Azure Bastion provides secure browser-based access to Azure VMs over the Azure portal without exposing RDP or SSH directly to the internet. This improves security by removing the need for public IP addresses on session hosts. Opening port 3389 publicly is risky and not recommended. RemoteApp is used for application publishing, not administration. Azure Bastion is commonly used for secure administrative access to session hosts.

Q11. What is the primary purpose of a host pool in Azure Virtual Desktop?

A. Store user data
B. Group session hosts for desktops/apps delivery
C. Manage DNS
D. Monitor performance

Answer: B. Group session hosts for desktops/apps delivery
Reasoning:
A host pool in Azure Virtual Desktop is a fundamental component that groups together multiple session hosts (virtual machines) to deliver desktops or RemoteApps to users. It acts as a logical container that defines how users connect, how sessions are distributed, and how resources are managed. Host pools enable administrators to configure load balancing methods, session limits, and scaling strategies efficiently. Without host pools, managing individual virtual machines would become complex and inefficient. The host pool abstracts the complexity of multiple VMs and provides a centralized way to manage them. It does not store user data, which is handled by storage solutions like Azure Files or Azure NetApp Files. It also does not directly manage DNS or monitoring, although it integrates with services that perform those functions.

Q12. Which load balancing method distributes sessions evenly across all session hosts?

A. Depth-first
B. Breadth-first
C. Round-robin
D. Sequential

Answer: B. Breadth-first
Reasoning:
Breadth-first load balancing distributes user sessions evenly across all available session hosts in a host pool. This ensures that no single host becomes overloaded while others remain underutilized. It is particularly useful in environments where maintaining consistent user experience is a priority, as it prevents performance degradation caused by uneven resource usage. In contrast, depth-first load balancing fills one session host to its maximum capacity before moving to the next, which is more cost-efficient but can lead to performance issues on heavily loaded machines. Breadth-first is ideal for scenarios where responsiveness and user satisfaction are more important than cost savings. It helps maintain stability, reduces the risk of bottlenecks, and ensures optimal use of all available compute resources.

Q13. What is the main purpose of FSLogix in Azure Virtual Desktop?

A. Manage networking
B. Store virtual machines
C. Manage user profiles
D. Monitor performance

Answer: C. Manage user profiles
Reasoning:
FSLogix is a profile management solution used in Azure Virtual Desktop to provide a consistent user experience across multiple session hosts. It stores user profiles in virtual hard disk (VHD/VHDX) files,

typically on Azure Files or Azure NetApp Files. When a user logs in, the profile container is dynamically attached to the session host, allowing the user to access their personalized settings, applications, and data regardless of which VM they connect to. This significantly reduces login times and eliminates issues related to roaming profiles or local profiles. FSLogix ensures that user environments remain consistent, even in pooled host environments where users may connect to different machines each time. It is essential for scalability and user satisfaction in enterprise AVD deployments.

Q14. What is the function of a workspace in Azure Virtual Desktop?

A. Store VMs
B. Provide a feed of resources to users
C. Manage DNS
D. Control storage

Answer: B. Provide a feed of resources to users
Reasoning:
A workspace in Azure Virtual Desktop acts as a container that aggregates application groups and presents them to users through the Remote Desktop client. When users subscribe to a workspace, they gain access to all desktops and applications assigned to them. This simplifies the user experience by providing a centralized location for accessing resources. Workspaces do not store virtual machines or manage storage directly. Instead, they serve as an interface between the user and the backend infrastructure. By organizing resources into workspaces, administrators can easily manage access and ensure users only see the applications and desktops relevant to them. This improves usability, security, and overall efficiency in resource delivery.

Q15. Which protocol is primarily used by Azure Virtual Desktop?

A. HTTP
B. SSH
C. RDP
D. FTP

Answer: C. RDP
Reasoning:
Azure Virtual Desktop relies on the Remote Desktop Protocol (RDP) to deliver desktops and applications to users. Microsoft has enhanced RDP for AVD by incorporating features such as reverse connect and RDP Shortpath, which improve security and performance. RDP enables efficient transmission of screen updates, keyboard input, and mouse actions between the client and the session host. Unlike HTTP or FTP, which are used for web and file transfer respectively, RDP is specifically designed for remote desktop access. SSH is typically used for secure command-line access to servers, not graphical desktops. RDP's optimization in AVD ensures low latency, high responsiveness, and a seamless user experience, even over varying network conditions.

Q16. What is reverse connect in Azure Virtual Desktop?

A. Direct user connection to VM
B. Session host initiates outbound connection
C. DNS routing

D. VPN connection

Answer: B. Session host initiates outbound connection
Reasoning:
Reverse connect is a key security feature in Azure Virtual Desktop that allows session hosts to establish outbound connections to the AVD service instead of requiring inbound connections from users. This eliminates the need to open inbound ports like 3389 (RDP) on virtual machines, significantly reducing the attack surface. Users connect to the AVD service, which then brokers the connection to the session host through this outbound channel. This approach enhances security by preventing direct exposure of VMs to the internet. It also simplifies network configuration, as administrators do not need to manage complex firewall rules or public IP addresses. Reverse connect is one of the reasons AVD is considered a secure remote desktop solution.

Q17. Which Azure service is commonly used to store FSLogix profiles?

A. Azure Monitor
B. Azure Files
C. Azure Policy
D. Azure DNS

Answer: B. Azure Files
Reasoning:
Azure Files is a fully managed file share service that supports SMB protocol, making it ideal for storing FSLogix profile containers. It allows multiple session hosts to access user profiles simultaneously, ensuring consistency across sessions. Azure Files integrates seamlessly with Azure Virtual Desktop and provides scalability, security, and high availability. While Azure NetApp Files is another option offering higher performance, Azure Files is more commonly used due to its cost-effectiveness and ease of deployment. Azure Monitor is used for monitoring, Azure Policy for governance, and Azure DNS for name resolution. Azure Files plays a critical role in enabling persistent user profiles in non-persistent AVD environments.

Q18. What is a session host in Azure Virtual Desktop?

A. User device
B. Virtual machine delivering desktop/app
C. Storage account
D. Monitoring tool

Answer: B. Virtual machine delivering desktop/app
Reasoning:
A session host is a virtual machine in Azure that runs the Azure Virtual Desktop agent and provides desktops or applications to users. It is the compute resource where user sessions are executed. Session hosts can be part of pooled or personal host pools, depending on the deployment model. They are responsible for processing user input, running applications, and delivering the graphical interface via RDP. Session hosts must be properly sized and configured to handle the expected number of users and workloads. They are central to the AVD architecture and directly impact performance and user experience. Storage accounts and monitoring tools support the environment but do not deliver user sessions.

Q19. What is session affinity in Azure Virtual Desktop?

A. Load balancing method
B. Reconnect user to same session
C. Storage feature
D. Security policy

Answer: B. Reconnect user to same session
Reasoning:
Session affinity ensures that when a user reconnects to Azure Virtual Desktop, they are directed back to their existing session rather than being assigned a new one. This is important for maintaining application state, unsaved work, and overall continuity. It improves user experience by preventing disruptions and ensuring consistency. Without session affinity, users might connect to a different session host and lose access to their previous session data. This feature is especially important in pooled environments where multiple users share session hosts. It works alongside load balancing to optimize both performance and user experience.

Q20. What is a personal host pool?

A. Shared desktops
B. Dedicated VM per user
C. Storage pool
D. Monitoring group

Answer: B. Dedicated VM per user
Reasoning:
A personal host pool assigns a dedicated virtual machine to each user, providing a persistent desktop experience. This means the user always connects to the same VM, allowing customization, application installation, and consistent settings. It is ideal for users who require administrative privileges or specialized configurations. Unlike pooled host pools, where multiple users share resources, personal host pools offer isolation and predictability. However, they are more expensive because each user requires a separate VM. This model is commonly used for developers, designers, or users with specific performance or security requirements. It provides a balance between flexibility and control, making it suitable for certain enterprise scenarios.

Q21. Which Azure role is required to manage Azure Virtual Desktop resources?

A. Reader
B. Owner
C. Desktop Virtualization Contributor
D. Security Reader

Answer: C. Desktop Virtualization Contributor
Reasoning:
The Desktop Virtualization Contributor role is specifically designed for managing Azure Virtual Desktop resources. It provides permissions to create, modify, and delete host pools, application groups, workspaces, and session hosts without granting full subscription-level control. While the Owner role

provides complete access, it is not recommended for regular operations due to security best practices like least privilege access. The Reader role only allows viewing resources and does not permit any changes. Security Reader is used for monitoring security configurations. Using a specialized role like Desktop Virtualization Contributor ensures administrators have just enough permissions to manage AVD infrastructure efficiently without exposing unnecessary risks, aligning with Azure's role-based access control (RBAC) model.

Q22. What is the purpose of autoscale in Azure Virtual Desktop?

A. Manage DNS
B. Automatically adjust VM capacity
C. Store user profiles
D. Encrypt data

Answer: B. Automatically adjust VM capacity
Reasoning:
Autoscale in Azure Virtual Desktop is used to dynamically start or stop session host virtual machines based on demand. This ensures that sufficient resources are available during peak usage while reducing costs during off-peak hours by shutting down unused VMs. Autoscale uses scaling plans based on schedules, session thresholds, and load balancing to optimize performance and cost. Without autoscale, administrators would need to manually manage VM availability, which can lead to inefficiencies. It does not manage DNS, store user profiles, or encrypt data. Instead, it plays a critical role in operational efficiency and cost management, making it an essential feature for enterprise AVD deployments.

Q23. Which authentication service is primarily used in Azure Virtual Desktop?

A. Active Directory only
B. Microsoft Entra ID
C. DNS
D. Azure Monitor

Answer: B. Microsoft Entra ID
Reasoning:
Microsoft Entra ID (formerly Azure Active Directory) is the primary identity and authentication service used in Azure Virtual Desktop. It allows users to securely sign in to their virtual desktops and applications. It also supports advanced features such as Conditional Access, Multi-Factor Authentication (MFA), and identity protection. While traditional Active Directory can still be used in hybrid environments, Entra ID is essential for cloud-native deployments. DNS is used for name resolution, and Azure Monitor is used for monitoring, not authentication. Entra ID ensures secure and scalable identity management, which is critical for modern cloud-based virtual desktop environments.

Q24. What improves login performance in Azure Virtual Desktop?

A. Increasing VM size only
B. Using FSLogix profile containers
C. Using DNS
D. Disabling autoscale

Answer: B. Using FSLogix profile containers
Reasoning:
FSLogix profile containers significantly improve login performance in Azure Virtual Desktop by storing user profiles in a virtual disk that is quickly mounted during login. This avoids delays associated with copying profile data across the network, which is common in traditional roaming profiles. FSLogix ensures faster logins and a consistent user experience, especially in pooled environments. While increasing VM size can help with performance, it does not directly address login delays. DNS and autoscale are unrelated to login performance. FSLogix is widely considered a best practice for optimizing user logon times and profile management in AVD.

Q25. What is the purpose of a session limit in a host pool?

A. Limit storage usage
B. Control maximum users per VM
C. Manage DNS
D. Monitor performance

Answer: B. Control maximum users per VM
Reasoning:
A session limit defines the maximum number of concurrent user sessions allowed on a single session host. This helps maintain performance and prevents overloading a virtual machine. By setting an appropriate session limit, administrators can ensure that each user gets sufficient resources such as CPU and memory. If too many users are allowed on a single VM, performance may degrade significantly. Session limits work together with load balancing to distribute users efficiently across hosts. This setting is critical in pooled host pools where multiple users share the same VM. It does not control storage, DNS, or monitoring directly.

Q26. Which feature allows users to access only specific applications instead of full desktops?

A. Desktop group
B. RemoteApp
C. Personal host pool
D. Azure Bastion

Answer: B. RemoteApp
Reasoning:
RemoteApp allows administrators to publish individual applications to users instead of providing full desktop access. This is useful when users only need access to specific business applications. It enhances security by limiting exposure to the full desktop environment and improves usability by simplifying the interface. Desktop groups provide full desktop access, while personal host pools assign dedicated VMs. Azure Bastion is used for secure administrative access and is unrelated to application delivery. RemoteApp is commonly used in enterprise environments to deliver applications efficiently while maintaining control and security.

Q27. What is Azure Bastion used for in AVD environments?

A. Monitor sessions
B. Secure VM access without public IP

C. Store profiles
D. Manage DNS

Answer: B. Secure VM access without public IP
Reasoning:
Azure Bastion provides secure, browser-based access to virtual machines without requiring a public IP address. This is important in AVD environments where exposing session hosts to the internet can create security risks. Bastion allows administrators to connect to VMs using RDP or SSH through the Azure portal over a secure connection. It eliminates the need to open inbound ports like 3389, reducing the attack surface. It does not monitor sessions, store profiles, or manage DNS. Azure Bastion is a key component for secure administrative access in cloud environments.

Q28. What is Conditional Access used for in Azure Virtual Desktop?

A. Load balancing
B. Security policy enforcement
C. Storage management
D. VM scaling

Answer: B. Security policy enforcement
Reasoning:
Conditional Access in Microsoft Entra ID allows administrators to enforce security policies based on user identity, device compliance, location, and risk level. In Azure Virtual Desktop, it ensures that only authorized users under specific conditions can access resources. For example, it can require Multi-Factor Authentication (MFA) or block access from certain locations. This enhances security by protecting sensitive data and preventing unauthorized access. Conditional Access is not used for load balancing, storage, or scaling. It is a critical component of identity and access management in modern cloud environments.

Q29. Which feature helps optimize network performance in AVD?

A. Azure Backup
B. RDP Shortpath
C. Azure Policy
D. Azure DNS

Answer: B. RDP Shortpath
Reasoning:
RDP Shortpath improves network performance by enabling a direct UDP-based connection between the client and the session host. This reduces latency and improves responsiveness, especially in environments with complex network routing. It bypasses some of the traditional relay infrastructure used in standard RDP connections. This results in better user experience, particularly for multimedia and real-time applications. Azure Backup, Azure Policy, and Azure DNS do not impact network performance in this way. RDP Shortpath is a key optimization feature in Azure Virtual Desktop.

Q30. What is Azure Virtual Desktop Insights used for?

A. Storage

B. Monitoring and diagnostics
C. Authentication
D. VM creation

Answer: B. Monitoring and diagnostics
Reasoning:
Azure Virtual Desktop Insights is a monitoring solution built on Azure Monitor and Log Analytics. It provides detailed information about session performance, connection health, host utilization, and user activity. Administrators can use it to identify issues, analyze trends, and optimize performance. It helps in troubleshooting problems such as slow logins, session drops, or resource bottlenecks. It does not handle storage, authentication, or VM creation. AVD Insights is essential for maintaining a healthy and efficient virtual desktop environment.

Q31. Which storage option provides the best performance for large-scale AVD deployments?

A. Azure Blob Storage
B. Azure Files Standard
C. Azure NetApp Files
D. Local Disk

Answer: C. Azure NetApp Files
Reasoning:
Azure NetApp Files is designed for high-performance workloads and is ideal for large-scale Azure Virtual Desktop deployments, especially when using FSLogix profile containers. It offers low latency, high throughput, and consistent performance, which are critical when many users log in simultaneously. Compared to Azure Files Standard, which is more cost-effective but has performance limitations, NetApp Files ensures faster profile load times and better user experience. Local disks are not suitable for shared profile storage, and Azure Blob Storage does not support SMB protocol required by FSLogix. In enterprise environments with hundreds or thousands of users, Azure NetApp Files helps avoid bottlenecks and ensures smooth operations. Although it is more expensive, the performance benefits often justify the cost for mission-critical workloads.

Q32. What is the main advantage of RDP Shortpath in AVD?

A. Reduces storage cost
B. Improves network latency
C. Increases VM size
D. Enhances authentication

Answer: B. Improves network latency
Reasoning:
RDP Shortpath enhances Azure Virtual Desktop performance by creating a direct UDP-based connection between the client and the session host. This reduces reliance on relay services and minimizes network hops, resulting in lower latency and improved responsiveness. It is especially beneficial for real-time applications like video conferencing, multimedia streaming, and interactive workloads. Unlike traditional TCP-based RDP connections, UDP provides better handling of packet loss and fluctuating network conditions. RDP Shortpath does not affect storage costs, VM sizing, or authentication directly. Instead, it

focuses on optimizing the network path, which is one of the most critical factors in delivering a smooth user experience in virtual desktop environments.

Q33. What are the two types of application groups in AVD?

A. Public and Private
B. Desktop and RemoteApp
C. Static and Dynamic
D. Internal and External

Answer: B. Desktop and RemoteApp
Reasoning:
Azure Virtual Desktop supports two types of application groups: Desktop and RemoteApp. Desktop application groups provide users with access to a full virtual desktop environment, while RemoteApp groups allow users to access individual applications without exposing the entire desktop. This flexibility enables organizations to tailor user access based on requirements. For example, employees who need a full workspace can use desktop groups, while others can access only specific business applications via RemoteApp. This improves security by limiting access and enhances usability by simplifying the interface. Other options like Public/Private or Static/Dynamic are not valid application group types in AVD. Understanding these two types is essential for designing efficient and secure virtual desktop solutions.

Q34. What is Azure Virtual Desktop Insights built on?

A. Azure DNS
B. Azure Monitor and Log Analytics
C. Azure Backup
D. Azure Policy

Answer: B. Azure Monitor and Log Analytics
Reasoning:
Azure Virtual Desktop Insights is built on Azure Monitor and Log Analytics, which together provide powerful monitoring and analytics capabilities. Azure Monitor collects metrics and logs from AVD resources, while Log Analytics allows querying and analyzing this data. AVD Insights uses pre-built workbooks to visualize performance data, session activity, connection reliability, and resource utilization. This helps administrators quickly identify issues and optimize the environment. Azure DNS, Backup, and Policy serve different purposes and are not used for monitoring AVD performance. By leveraging Azure Monitor and Log Analytics, AVD Insights provides deep visibility into the virtual desktop infrastructure.

Q35. Which operating system supports multi-session in AVD?

A. Windows Server 2016
B. Windows 10/11 Enterprise multi-session
C. Linux
D. macOS

Answer: B. Windows 10/11 Enterprise multi-session
Reasoning:

Windows 10/11 Enterprise multi-session is specifically designed for Azure Virtual Desktop and allows multiple users to share a single virtual machine simultaneously. This significantly reduces infrastructure costs compared to assigning one VM per user. It provides a familiar desktop experience while maintaining efficiency and scalability. Windows Server also supports multi-user sessions, but Windows Enterprise multi-session is optimized for AVD and offers better integration with modern desktop environments. Linux and macOS are not supported as session host operating systems in AVD. This OS is a key innovation that makes Azure Virtual Desktop cost-effective and scalable.

Q36. What is the purpose of scaling plans in AVD?

A. Manage DNS
B. Control VM start/stop schedules
C. Store profiles
D. Monitor performance

Answer: B. Control VM start/stop schedules
Reasoning:
Scaling plans in Azure Virtual Desktop are used to automate the starting and stopping of session host virtual machines based on predefined schedules and usage patterns. This helps optimize costs by ensuring that VMs are only running when needed. For example, during business hours, more session hosts can be active, while during off-hours, unused VMs can be shut down. Scaling plans also help maintain performance by ensuring sufficient capacity during peak times. They do not manage DNS, store profiles, or directly monitor performance. Instead, they play a crucial role in balancing cost efficiency and resource availability.

Q37. Which disk type is recommended for high-performance AVD workloads?

A. Standard HDD
B. Standard SSD
C. Premium SSD
D. Archive Storage

Answer: C. Premium SSD
Reasoning:
Premium SSDs provide high IOPS and low latency, making them ideal for Azure Virtual Desktop workloads that require fast data access. Session hosts rely on disk performance for OS operations, application loading, and temporary data storage. Using Premium SSD ensures smooth performance and reduces delays experienced by users. Standard HDDs are slower and not suitable for performance-sensitive workloads. Standard SSDs offer moderate performance but may not meet enterprise requirements. Archive storage is used for long-term data retention and is not suitable for active workloads. Choosing the right disk type is essential for delivering a responsive user experience in AVD.

Q38. What problem does FSLogix solve in AVD?

A. Network latency
B. Profile consistency
C. DNS issues
D. VM scaling

Answer: B. Profile consistency
Reasoning:
FSLogix solves the problem of inconsistent user profiles in multi-session environments by storing profiles in containers that can be attached to any session host. This ensures that users have the same settings, files, and applications regardless of which VM they connect to. Without FSLogix, users might experience missing data or inconsistent environments when switching session hosts. It does not directly address network latency, DNS issues, or VM scaling. Instead, it focuses on providing a seamless and consistent user experience, which is critical in enterprise deployments.

Q39. What is a key security best practice for AVD session hosts?

A. Assign public IPs
B. Disable encryption
C. Remove public IPs
D. Use FTP

Answer: C. Remove public IPs
Reasoning:
Removing public IP addresses from session hosts is a critical security best practice in Azure Virtual Desktop. This prevents direct exposure of VMs to the internet, reducing the risk of attacks such as brute force or unauthorized access. Instead, secure access methods like Azure Bastion or VPN should be used. Assigning public IPs increases vulnerability, while disabling encryption and using FTP are insecure practices. By minimizing exposure and using secure access methods, organizations can significantly enhance the security posture of their AVD environment.

Q40. Which feature protects data stored on AVD disks?

A. Azure Disk Encryption
B. Azure Monitor
C. Azure DNS
D. Azure Policy

Answer: A. Azure Disk Encryption
Reasoning:
Azure Disk Encryption protects data at rest by encrypting virtual machine disks using industry-standard encryption technologies. This ensures that sensitive data stored on AVD session hosts remains secure even if the underlying storage is compromised. It integrates with Azure Key Vault to manage encryption keys securely. Azure Monitor is used for monitoring, DNS for name resolution, and Policy for governance. Encryption is a critical component of data security and compliance, making Azure Disk Encryption an essential feature in Azure Virtual Desktop environments.

Q41. What is the most important factor to consider when choosing an Azure region for AVD deployment?

A. Cost only
B. Proximity to users
C. Number of VMs

D. Storage size

Answer: B. Proximity to users
Reasoning:
When selecting an Azure region for Azure Virtual Desktop, the most critical factor is proximity to users. The closer the Azure region is to the end users, the lower the network latency, which directly improves responsiveness and overall user experience. AVD relies heavily on real-time communication between the user device and the session host, so even small delays can impact performance. While cost and resource availability are also important, they should not come at the expense of performance. Choosing a distant region may reduce costs slightly but can result in poor user experience. Therefore, organizations should prioritize regions closest to their user base while balancing compliance, availability, and pricing considerations.

Q42. What is the purpose of the Azure Virtual Desktop agent?

A. Store user data
B. Enable communication between VM and AVD service
C. Manage DNS
D. Encrypt disks

Answer: B. Enable communication between VM and AVD service
Reasoning:
The Azure Virtual Desktop agent is a critical component installed on each session host VM. It enables communication between the virtual machine and the Azure Virtual Desktop service. The agent registers the VM with the host pool, allows it to receive connection requests, and ensures proper functioning of sessions. Without the agent, the VM cannot participate in the AVD environment. It does not store user data, manage DNS, or handle encryption. Instead, it acts as the bridge that connects the infrastructure (VMs) to the AVD control plane. Keeping the agent updated is essential for security, compatibility, and performance improvements.

Q43. What happens when a user subscribes to a workspace?

A. VM is created
B. User receives assigned desktops/apps
C. Storage is allocated
D. DNS is configured

Answer: B. User receives assigned desktops/apps
Reasoning:
When a user subscribes to a workspace in Azure Virtual Desktop, they gain access to the desktops and applications assigned to them through application groups. The workspace acts as a delivery mechanism, presenting these resources in the Remote Desktop client. This simplifies access, as users do not need to manually configure connections. Instead, they see all available resources in one place. Subscribing to a workspace does not create virtual machines, allocate storage, or configure DNS. It is purely a user-facing feature that improves usability and resource discovery. This mechanism ensures that users can easily access the tools they need without complex setup.

Q44. Which strategy helps reduce AVD operational costs?

A. Increase VM size
B. Use autoscaling and reserved instances
C. Disable monitoring
D. Use public IPs

Answer: B. Use autoscaling and reserved instances
Reasoning:
Cost optimization in Azure Virtual Desktop is achieved by combining autoscaling and reserved instances. Autoscaling ensures that session hosts are only running when needed, reducing unnecessary compute costs. Reserved instances provide discounted pricing for long-term VM usage, making them ideal for predictable workloads. Increasing VM size unnecessarily raises costs, while disabling monitoring can lead to inefficiencies and undetected issues. Using public IPs does not reduce costs and may increase security risks. By carefully managing resource usage and leveraging Azure pricing models, organizations can significantly reduce operational expenses while maintaining performance and availability.

Q45. What should you check first if users experience slow login times?

A. DNS settings
B. FSLogix configuration
C. VM name
D. Subscription ID

Answer: B. FSLogix configuration
Reasoning:
Slow login times in Azure Virtual Desktop are often related to profile loading issues, making FSLogix configuration the first thing to check. FSLogix manages user profiles and ensures they are quickly mounted during login. If misconfigured, profiles may take longer to load or fail entirely, causing delays. Other factors like DNS or VM naming are less likely to impact login performance directly. Ensuring proper storage performance, network connectivity, and FSLogix settings is essential for optimizing login times. Monitoring tools like Azure Monitor can also help identify bottlenecks. Proper configuration of FSLogix is critical for delivering a smooth and efficient user experience.

Q46. Which service is used to sync on-premises AD with Azure?

A. Azure Monitor
B. Microsoft Entra Connect
C. Azure DNS
D. Azure Backup

Answer: B. Microsoft Entra Connect
Reasoning:
Microsoft Entra Connect (formerly Azure AD Connect) is used to synchronize identities between on-premises Active Directory and Microsoft Entra ID. This allows users to use the same credentials across both environments, enabling hybrid identity scenarios. In Azure Virtual Desktop, this is important for organizations that still rely on on-premises infrastructure. Entra Connect ensures consistency, simplifies authentication, and supports features like single sign-on (SSO). Azure Monitor, DNS, and Backup serve

different purposes and are not used for identity synchronization. Entra Connect is a key component in hybrid cloud environments.

Q47. What is Azure Compute Gallery used for?

A. Monitoring
B. Image management and distribution
C. DNS
D. Backup

Answer: B. Image management and distribution
Reasoning:
Azure Compute Gallery (formerly Shared Image Gallery) is used to store, manage, and distribute custom VM images across Azure regions. In AVD, it allows administrators to create standardized images with pre-installed applications and configurations. This ensures consistency across session hosts and simplifies deployment. It also supports versioning and replication, making it easier to scale environments. Monitoring, DNS, and backup are handled by other services. Using Azure Compute Gallery improves efficiency, reduces deployment time, and ensures that all session hosts are configured identically.

Q48. Which service provides logging for AVD?

A. Azure Monitor
B. Azure Files
C. Azure Bastion
D. Azure Policy

Answer: A. Azure Monitor
Reasoning:
Azure Monitor collects logs and metrics from Azure Virtual Desktop resources, providing visibility into system performance and user activity. It integrates with Log Analytics to allow detailed querying and analysis of data. This helps administrators troubleshoot issues, monitor usage, and optimize performance. Azure Files stores data, Bastion provides secure access, and Policy enforces governance rules. Logging is essential for maintaining a reliable and secure AVD environment, making Azure Monitor a critical service.

Q49. What is RBAC used for in AVD?

A. Storage
B. Access control
C. Networking
D. Backup

Answer: B. Access control
Reasoning:
Role-Based Access Control (RBAC) in Azure is used to manage who can access and modify resources. In Azure Virtual Desktop, RBAC ensures that only authorized users can perform specific actions, such as managing host pools or assigning applications. It follows the principle of least privilege, reducing security risks by limiting access to only what is necessary. RBAC does not handle storage, networking, or backup

directly. It is a fundamental security feature that helps organizations maintain control over their cloud resources.

Q50. Which service is used to back up AVD virtual machines?

A. Azure Monitor
B. Azure Backup
C. Azure DNS
D. Azure Policy

Answer: B. Azure Backup
Reasoning:
Azure Backup is used to protect virtual machines by creating recovery points that can be used to restore data in case of failure, corruption, or accidental deletion. In Azure Virtual Desktop, backing up session hosts and related resources ensures business continuity and disaster recovery. Azure Monitor tracks performance, DNS manages name resolution, and Policy enforces compliance. Backup is essential for protecting critical workloads and ensuring that data can be recovered quickly in case of issues. Azure Backup provides a reliable and scalable solution for this purpose.

Q51. What should you do if session hosts are running at high CPU usage?

A. Delete VMs
B. Increase VM size or add more hosts
C. Disable users
D. Change DNS

Answer: B. Increase VM size or add more hosts
Reasoning:
High CPU usage on session hosts indicates that the current resources are insufficient to handle the workload. The best approach is to either scale up (increase VM size) or scale out (add more session hosts). Scaling up provides more CPU and memory to handle intensive workloads, while scaling out distributes users across multiple machines, reducing the load on each host. This ensures better performance and user experience. Deleting VMs or disabling users is not a practical solution and may disrupt operations. DNS changes do not affect CPU performance. Proper capacity planning, combined with autoscaling, helps maintain optimal performance and prevents resource bottlenecks in Azure Virtual Desktop environments.

Q52. What is the best solution for high network latency in AVD?

A. Increase storage
B. Use a closer Azure region
C. Increase VM size
D. Disable FSLogix

Answer: B. Use a closer Azure region
Reasoning:
Network latency directly impacts the responsiveness of Azure Virtual Desktop sessions. The most effective way to reduce latency is to deploy session hosts in an Azure region closer to the end users. This minimizes the physical distance data must travel, resulting in faster response times. Increasing storage or VM size does not address latency issues, and disabling FSLogix would negatively affect user experience. Additionally, using features like RDP Shortpath and optimizing network routes can further improve performance. Choosing the right region during the design phase is one of the most important decisions for ensuring a smooth and responsive virtual desktop experience.

Q53. What is a common cause of session disconnections in AVD?

A. Storage size
B. Network instability
C. VM name
D. Disk type

Answer: B. Network instability
Reasoning:
Session disconnections in Azure Virtual Desktop are most commonly caused by network instability. Since AVD relies on continuous communication between the user device and the session host, any interruptions in connectivity can result in session drops. Factors such as poor internet connection, packet loss, or high latency can disrupt the session. Storage size, VM name, and disk type do not directly affect

session stability. To resolve such issues, administrators should analyze network performance, use tools like Azure Monitor, and implement optimizations such as RDP Shortpath. Ensuring a stable and high-quality network connection is essential for maintaining uninterrupted user sessions.

Q54. How do you fix a corrupted FSLogix profile?

A. Restart VM
B. Reset or recreate profile container
C. Change DNS
D. Increase CPU

Answer: B. Reset or recreate profile container
Reasoning:
When an FSLogix profile becomes corrupted, users may experience login failures or missing data. The recommended solution is to reset or recreate the profile container. This involves deleting or renaming the corrupted VHD/VHDX file so that a new profile can be created during the next login. Restarting the VM or increasing CPU will not resolve profile corruption. DNS changes are also unrelated. While recreating the profile may result in loss of user-specific settings, it restores functionality and allows users to log in successfully. Proper backup and monitoring can help prevent data loss and detect issues early.

Q55. What should you check if users cannot access a published application?

A. Disk type
B. Application group assignment
C. VM size
D. DNS

Answer: B. Application group assignment
Reasoning:
If users cannot access a published application in Azure Virtual Desktop, the first thing to check is whether they are assigned to the correct application group. Application groups control access to desktops and RemoteApps, and users must be explicitly assigned to them. If the assignment is missing or incorrect, the application will not appear in the user's workspace. Disk type, VM size, and DNS settings do not directly affect application visibility. Ensuring proper user assignment is a fundamental step in troubleshooting access issues. Administrators should also verify workspace subscriptions and permissions to ensure proper access.

Q56. What should you verify if a user cannot log in to AVD?

A. Disk size
B. RBAC and Entra ID permissions
C. VM color
D. Storage account name

Answer: B. RBAC and Entra ID permissions
Reasoning:
User login issues in Azure Virtual Desktop are often related to identity and access permissions. Administrators should verify that the user is correctly authenticated in Microsoft Entra ID and has the

necessary role assignments (RBAC) to access AVD resources. If permissions are missing or misconfigured, the user will be unable to log in. Disk size, VM color, and storage account names do not impact authentication. Ensuring proper identity configuration, group membership, and application group assignment is essential for successful login. Conditional Access policies should also be reviewed if they are in place.

Q57. What should you do if a VM is underperforming?

A. Rename VM
B. Upgrade VM SKU
C. Change DNS
D. Delete storage

Answer: B. Upgrade VM SKU
Reasoning:
If a session host VM is underperforming, upgrading the VM SKU (size) is a practical solution. This provides more CPU, memory, and resources to handle user workloads. Underperformance can result from insufficient resources, especially when multiple users share the same VM. Renaming the VM or changing DNS does not impact performance. Deleting storage can cause data loss and is not a solution. Proper monitoring using Azure Monitor can help identify performance bottlenecks, and scaling strategies can be implemented to maintain optimal performance in Azure Virtual Desktop environments.

Q58. Which feature is used to create alerts for AVD issues?

A. Azure Monitor alerts
B. Azure DNS
C. Azure Files
D. Azure Policy

Answer: A. Azure Monitor alerts
Reasoning:
Azure Monitor alerts allow administrators to proactively detect and respond to issues in Azure Virtual Desktop. Alerts can be configured based on metrics such as CPU usage, session count, or connection failures. When thresholds are exceeded, notifications are sent, enabling quick action. This helps maintain system health and prevent downtime. Azure DNS, Files, and Policy do not provide alerting capabilities. Monitoring and alerting are essential for maintaining a reliable and efficient AVD environment.

Q59. What should you do if CPU usage is consistently high across all hosts?

A. Reduce users
B. Scale out session hosts
C. Disable monitoring
D. Change DNS

Answer: B. Scale out session hosts
Reasoning:
Consistently high CPU usage across all session hosts indicates that the environment is under-provisioned. The best solution is to scale out by adding more session hosts to distribute the load. This reduces the

number of users per VM and improves performance. Reducing users is not practical, and disabling monitoring would hide the problem. DNS changes do not affect CPU usage. Scaling out ensures better resource utilization and enhances user experience. Combining this with autoscaling can help maintain optimal performance dynamically.

Q60. What is the most important design principle for AVD?

A. Color scheme
B. Scalability, security, and cost optimization
C. VM naming
D. Disk labeling

Answer: B. Scalability, security, and cost optimization
Reasoning:
The most important design principle for Azure Virtual Desktop is balancing scalability, security, and cost optimization. AVD environments must be able to scale to meet user demand, ensure data and access security, and remain cost-effective. Scalability ensures that resources can grow or shrink based on usage. Security protects sensitive data and prevents unauthorized access. Cost optimization ensures efficient use of resources and budget. Other factors like naming or labeling are important for organization but do not impact overall system design. A well-designed AVD solution considers all three aspects to deliver a reliable and efficient virtual desktop experience.

Q61. What is the purpose of Start VM on Connect in Azure Virtual Desktop?

A. Shut down VMs automatically
B. Start session hosts when users connect
C. Manage DNS
D. Store user data

Answer: B. Start session hosts when users connect
Reasoning:
Start VM on Connect is a feature in Azure Virtual Desktop that automatically starts a session host virtual machine when a user attempts to connect. This helps reduce costs by allowing VMs to remain stopped when not in use, while still ensuring availability when users need access. It is especially useful in personal host pool scenarios or environments with predictable usage patterns. Without this feature, administrators would need to keep VMs running continuously or manually start them, leading to increased operational overhead and cost. This feature improves efficiency by balancing cost savings with user accessibility. It does not manage DNS or store user data, but instead focuses on optimizing compute resource usage.

Q62. Which feature ensures secure access based on device compliance?

A. Azure Backup
B. Conditional Access
C. Azure DNS
D. Azure Files

Answer: B. Conditional Access

Reasoning:
Conditional Access in Microsoft Entra ID allows administrators to enforce access policies based on conditions such as device compliance, location, and user risk level. In Azure Virtual Desktop, this ensures that only devices meeting security requirements can access resources. For example, access can be restricted to devices that are compliant with Intune policies or require Multi-Factor Authentication. This enhances security by preventing unauthorized or risky access attempts. Azure Backup, DNS, and Files do not provide access control capabilities. Conditional Access is a critical component of modern identity security, helping organizations enforce strict access policies while maintaining flexibility and usability.

Q63. What is the benefit of using managed identities in AVD?

A. Reduce storage cost
B. Secure access to Azure resources without credentials
C. Improve network speed
D. Increase VM size

Answer: B. Secure access to Azure resources without credentials
Reasoning:
Managed identities allow Azure Virtual Desktop session hosts to securely access other Azure services without storing credentials in code or configuration files. This eliminates the need for managing secrets, reducing the risk of credential exposure. For example, a session host can use a managed identity to access Azure Key Vault or storage accounts securely. This improves security and simplifies identity management. Managed identities do not impact storage cost, network speed, or VM size directly. They are part of Azure's identity and security framework, enabling secure and seamless integration between services.

Q64. What is the purpose of Azure Policy in AVD?

A. Monitor sessions
B. Enforce compliance and governance
C. Store profiles
D. Manage DNS

Answer: B. Enforce compliance and governance
Reasoning:
Azure Policy is used to enforce organizational standards and compliance requirements across Azure resources, including Azure Virtual Desktop. It allows administrators to define rules that ensure resources are configured correctly, such as requiring encryption, restricting regions, or enforcing naming conventions. This helps maintain consistency and security across deployments. Azure Policy does not directly monitor sessions or store profiles, but it ensures that the environment adheres to best practices and regulatory requirements. It is an essential tool for governance in enterprise environments.

Q65. Which feature helps distribute traffic across session hosts efficiently?

A. Azure Backup
B. Load balancing
C. Azure DNS
D. Azure Files

Answer: B. Load balancing
Reasoning:
Load balancing in Azure Virtual Desktop ensures that user sessions are distributed efficiently across available session hosts. This prevents any single host from becoming overloaded while others remain underutilized. It improves performance, reliability, and user experience. AVD supports different load balancing methods such as breadth-first and depth-first, allowing administrators to choose based on performance or cost optimization needs. Azure Backup, DNS, and Files do not perform this function. Load balancing is a core feature that ensures optimal resource utilization and system stability.

Q66. What is the purpose of host pool registration token?

A. Authenticate users
B. Register session hosts to host pool
C. Manage storage
D. Monitor performance

Answer: B. Register session hosts to host pool
Reasoning:
A host pool registration token is used to securely add new session host virtual machines to an Azure Virtual Desktop host pool. When deploying a VM, the token ensures that the VM is authorized to join the host pool and communicate with the AVD service. This process is essential for scaling and adding new resources. The token has a limited validity period for security reasons. It does not authenticate end users, manage storage, or monitor performance. Proper handling of registration tokens is important to maintain a secure environment.

Q67. Which tool is used to manage updates on AVD session hosts?

A. Azure Update Management
B. Azure DNS
C. Azure Files
D. Azure Bastion

Answer: A. Azure Update Management
Reasoning:
Azure Update Management is used to manage and automate operating system updates for virtual machines, including AVD session hosts. Keeping session hosts updated is critical for security, performance, and compliance. Update Management allows administrators to schedule updates, track compliance, and ensure that all VMs are running the latest patches. This reduces vulnerabilities and improves system stability. DNS, Files, and Bastion do not handle updates. Regular patching is a key operational task in maintaining a secure and efficient AVD environment.

Q68. What is the purpose of FSLogix Office container?

A. Store VM images
B. Optimize Office 365 performance
C. Manage DNS
D. Scale VMs

Answer: B. Optimize Office 365 performance
Reasoning:
FSLogix Office containers are used to improve the performance of Microsoft 365 applications in Azure Virtual Desktop environments. They store Office-related data such as Outlook OST files separately from the main profile container. This reduces login times and improves application responsiveness, especially in multi-session environments. Without Office containers, large Outlook files can slow down profile loading and impact performance. This feature is essential for organizations using Microsoft 365 in AVD. It does not manage DNS or scale VMs but focuses on optimizing application performance.

Q69. Which feature allows persistent desktop assignment in pooled host pools?

A. Load balancing
B. Personal assignment
C. FSLogix
D. Autoscale

Answer: B. Personal assignment
Reasoning:
Personal assignment allows users in a pooled host pool to consistently connect to the same session host, providing a semi-persistent experience. This is useful when users need some level of consistency without requiring a full personal host pool. It combines the benefits of pooled environments (cost efficiency) with elements of persistence. Load balancing distributes sessions, FSLogix manages profiles, and autoscale manages VM capacity. Personal assignment helps improve user experience by maintaining familiarity and reducing variability between sessions.

Q70. What is the purpose of Azure Key Vault in AVD?

A. Store user profiles
B. Securely store secrets and keys
C. Manage DNS
D. Monitor performance

Answer: B. Securely store secrets and keys
Reasoning:
Azure Key Vault is used to securely store and manage sensitive information such as passwords, certificates, and encryption keys. In Azure Virtual Desktop, it can be used to store secrets required by applications or automation scripts. This enhances security by eliminating the need to hardcode credentials. Key Vault integrates with managed identities to provide secure access without exposing secrets. It does not store user profiles, manage DNS, or monitor performance. Using Key Vault is a best practice for securing sensitive data in cloud environments.

Q71. What is the purpose of Azure AD Domain Services (AAD DS) in AVD?

A. Monitor sessions
B. Provide domain services without on-prem AD
C. Store profiles
D. Manage DNS

Answer: B. Provide domain services without on-prem AD
Reasoning:
Azure AD Domain Services (AAD DS) provides managed domain services such as domain join, Group Policy, LDAP, and Kerberos authentication without requiring on-premises Active Directory. In Azure Virtual Desktop, it is useful when organizations want to deploy session hosts in a cloud-only environment while still needing traditional domain services. AAD DS simplifies infrastructure by eliminating the need to deploy and manage domain controllers in Azure. It integrates with Microsoft Entra ID, allowing users to authenticate using cloud identities. It does not directly monitor sessions or store profiles, but it plays a critical role in enabling domain-based authentication and policy enforcement in AVD environments.

Q72. What is the benefit of using proximity placement groups (PPG) in AVD?

A. Reduce storage cost
B. Reduce network latency between VMs
C. Increase VM size
D. Manage DNS

Answer: B. Reduce network latency between VMs
Reasoning:
Proximity Placement Groups ensure that virtual machines are physically located close to each other within the same Azure datacenter. In Azure Virtual Desktop, this reduces latency between session hosts and supporting services such as domain controllers or file servers. Lower latency improves performance, especially for profile loading and authentication. This is particularly important in large deployments where multiple components interact frequently. PPG does not reduce storage cost or increase VM size, but it optimizes communication efficiency. It is a useful design consideration for performance-sensitive workloads.

Q73. Which feature is used to isolate network traffic in AVD?

A. Azure Backup
B. Virtual Network (VNet)
C. Azure Monitor
D. Azure Policy

Answer: B. Virtual Network (VNet)
Reasoning:
A Virtual Network (VNet) in Azure provides network isolation and segmentation for resources, including AVD session hosts. It allows administrators to define IP address ranges, subnets, and security rules. VNets ensure that traffic between session hosts, domain controllers, and storage services remains secure and private. They also enable integration with on-premises networks through VPN or ExpressRoute. Azure Backup, Monitor, and Policy do not provide network isolation. VNets are a fundamental component of Azure networking and are essential for securing and organizing AVD environments.

Q74. What is the purpose of Network Security Groups (NSG) in AVD?

A. Store profiles
B. Control inbound and outbound traffic

C. Monitor sessions
D. Manage DNS

Answer: B. Control inbound and outbound traffic
Reasoning:
Network Security Groups (NSGs) are used to define security rules that control inbound and outbound traffic to Azure resources. In Azure Virtual Desktop, NSGs help protect session hosts by allowing only necessary traffic and blocking unauthorized access. For example, administrators can restrict access to specific ports or IP ranges. NSGs enhance security by enforcing network-level protection. They do not store profiles or monitor sessions, but they are essential for securing communication within the AVD environment. Proper NSG configuration is critical to maintaining a secure deployment.

Q75. What is the purpose of Azure Firewall in AVD?

A. Store data
B. Provide advanced network security
C. Manage profiles
D. Monitor performance

Answer: B. Provide advanced network security
Reasoning:
Azure Firewall is a managed network security service that provides centralized control over network traffic. In Azure Virtual Desktop, it can be used to protect session hosts and other resources by filtering traffic based on rules and policies. It supports features such as application filtering, threat intelligence, and logging. Azure Firewall adds an additional layer of security beyond NSGs, especially in complex environments. It does not store data or manage profiles, but it plays a key role in securing network communication and preventing unauthorized access.

Q76. Which service helps integrate on-premises network with AVD?

A. Azure Monitor
B. VPN Gateway
C. Azure Files
D. Azure Policy

Answer: B. VPN Gateway
Reasoning:
VPN Gateway enables secure connectivity between on-premises networks and Azure Virtual Networks. In Azure Virtual Desktop, this allows session hosts to communicate with on-premises resources such as domain controllers or file servers. It is essential for hybrid deployments where organizations maintain both cloud and on-premises infrastructure. Azure Monitor, Files, and Policy do not provide network connectivity. VPN Gateway ensures secure and reliable communication, making it a critical component in hybrid AVD environments.

Q77. What is ExpressRoute used for in AVD?

A. Backup
B. Private dedicated network connection
C. DNS management
D. VM scaling

Answer: B. Private dedicated network connection
Reasoning:
ExpressRoute provides a private, dedicated connection between on-premises infrastructure and Azure. In Azure Virtual Desktop, it offers higher reliability, lower latency, and better security compared to public internet connections. This is particularly important for enterprise environments with strict performance and compliance requirements. ExpressRoute bypasses the public internet, reducing exposure to threats and improving consistency. It does not handle backup, DNS, or scaling directly. It is a premium networking solution for organizations that require high-performance connectivity.

Q78. What is the purpose of FSLogix redirections.xml?

A. Store VM images
B. Exclude folders from profile container
C. Manage DNS
D. Scale VMs

Answer: B. Exclude folders from profile container
Reasoning:
The redirections.xml file in FSLogix is used to exclude specific folders from being included in the profile container. This helps reduce profile size and improve performance by avoiding unnecessary data storage. For example, temporary files or cache data can be excluded. Smaller profiles load faster and consume less storage. This feature is important for optimizing FSLogix performance in Azure Virtual Desktop. It does not store VM images or manage DNS, but it plays a key role in efficient profile management.

Q79. Which feature helps optimize storage cost in AVD?

A. Premium SSD only
B. Azure Files lifecycle management
C. Increase VM size
D. Disable FSLogix

Answer: B. Azure Files lifecycle management
Reasoning:
Azure Files lifecycle management helps optimize storage costs by automatically moving data to lower-cost tiers based on usage patterns. In Azure Virtual Desktop, this is useful for managing FSLogix profile data efficiently. Frequently accessed data remains in high-performance tiers, while less frequently accessed data can be moved to cheaper storage. This reduces overall storage costs without impacting performance significantly. Increasing VM size or disabling FSLogix does not optimize storage costs. Lifecycle management is an effective way to balance performance and cost.

Q80. What is the purpose of session timeout settings in AVD?

A. Increase VM size
B. Disconnect idle sessions
C. Manage DNS
D. Store data

Answer: B. Disconnect idle sessions
Reasoning:
Session timeout settings in Azure Virtual Desktop are used to automatically disconnect or log off idle user sessions after a specified period. This helps free up resources and improve overall system efficiency. Idle sessions consume CPU, memory, and licensing resources, which can impact performance and increase costs. By configuring timeouts, administrators can ensure that resources are available for active users. This feature does not increase VM size, manage DNS, or store data. It is an important tool for optimizing resource utilization and maintaining a responsive environment.

Q81. What is the purpose of draining mode in Azure Virtual Desktop?

A. Delete sessions
B. Prevent new sessions on a host
C. Increase VM size
D. Manage DNS

Answer: B. Prevent new sessions on a host
Reasoning:
Draining mode is used in Azure Virtual Desktop to prevent new user sessions from being assigned to a specific session host while allowing existing sessions to continue until users log off. This is especially useful during maintenance activities such as updates, troubleshooting, or decommissioning a VM. By enabling drain mode, administrators can safely take a host out of rotation without disrupting active users. Once all sessions are closed, the VM can be shut down or modified. Draining mode does not delete sessions or affect DNS. It is an important operational feature that ensures smooth maintenance with minimal impact on user productivity and system availability.

Q82. Which feature helps reduce login storm impact in AVD?

A. Increase DNS
B. FSLogix + proper scaling
C. Disable users
D. Reduce storage

Answer: B. FSLogix + proper scaling
Reasoning:
A login storm occurs when many users attempt to log in simultaneously, often at the start of a workday. This can strain resources such as CPU, memory, and storage. Using FSLogix ensures that user profiles load efficiently, while proper scaling ensures that enough session hosts are available to handle the demand. Together, these strategies reduce login delays and prevent performance degradation. Increasing DNS or reducing storage does not address the issue, and disabling users is not a viable solution. Proper planning, autoscaling, and optimized profile management are key to handling login storms effectively.

Q83. What is the purpose of a golden image in AVD?

A. Backup
B. Standardized VM template
C. DNS configuration
D. Monitoring

Answer: B. Standardized VM template
Reasoning:
A golden image is a pre-configured virtual machine image that includes the operating system, applications, and settings required for Azure Virtual Desktop session hosts. It ensures consistency across all deployed VMs, reducing configuration errors and deployment time. Administrators can update the golden image and redeploy session hosts to apply changes across the environment. This approach simplifies management and improves reliability. Golden images are typically stored in Azure Compute Gallery for easy distribution. They do not directly handle backup, DNS, or monitoring, but they are essential for efficient and scalable AVD deployments.

Q84. Which feature helps manage application updates in AVD?

A. Azure Backup
B. Image update strategy
C. Azure DNS
D. Azure Files

Answer: B. Image update strategy
Reasoning:
Managing application updates in Azure Virtual Desktop is typically done through an image update strategy. Administrators update the golden image with new applications or patches and then redeploy session hosts using the updated image. This ensures consistency and reduces manual effort. This approach is more efficient than updating each VM individually. Azure Backup, DNS, and Files do not

manage application updates. Using a structured image update strategy helps maintain a secure, up-to-date, and consistent environment across all session hosts.

Q85. What is the benefit of using Intune with AVD?

A. Storage management
B. Device management and compliance
C. DNS control
D. VM scaling

Answer: B. Device management and compliance
Reasoning:
Microsoft Intune is used for device management and compliance in Azure Virtual Desktop environments. It allows administrators to enforce policies, manage updates, and ensure that devices accessing AVD meet security requirements. Intune integrates with Conditional Access to restrict access based on device compliance. This enhances security by ensuring that only trusted devices can connect to virtual desktops. Intune does not manage storage, DNS, or VM scaling, but it plays a critical role in endpoint security and governance.

Q86. Which feature improves multimedia performance in AVD?

A. Azure Backup
B. Multimedia redirection
C. Azure Policy
D. Azure DNS

Answer: B. Multimedia redirection
Reasoning:
Multimedia redirection improves performance in Azure Virtual Desktop by offloading video and audio processing to the client device instead of the session host. This reduces CPU usage on the VM and improves playback quality. It is especially useful for applications like Microsoft Teams or streaming services. Without multimedia redirection, session hosts may become overloaded, leading to poor performance. Azure Backup, Policy, and DNS do not impact multimedia performance. This feature enhances user experience and optimizes resource utilization.

Q87. What is the purpose of Teams optimization in AVD?

A. Backup data
B. Improve Teams performance
C. Manage DNS
D. Scale VMs

Answer: B. Improve Teams performance
Reasoning:
Microsoft Teams optimization in Azure Virtual Desktop ensures that audio and video processing is handled locally on the client device rather than on the session host. This reduces latency, improves call quality, and lowers resource usage on the VM. Without optimization, Teams performance may be poor due to high CPU and bandwidth requirements. This feature is essential for organizations that rely on

collaboration tools. It does not handle backup, DNS, or scaling, but it significantly enhances the user experience in AVD environments.

Q88. Which feature helps monitor user sessions in real time?

A. Azure Monitor
B. Azure Files
C. Azure DNS
D. Azure Backup

Answer: A. Azure Monitor
Reasoning:
Azure Monitor provides real-time insights into user sessions, performance metrics, and system health in Azure Virtual Desktop. It allows administrators to track active sessions, identify issues, and analyze trends. This helps in troubleshooting and optimizing the environment. Azure Files stores data, DNS handles name resolution, and Backup protects data. Monitoring is essential for maintaining system reliability and ensuring a smooth user experience. Azure Monitor is the primary tool for this purpose.

Q89. What is the purpose of user profile disks in AVD (legacy concept)?

A. Store OS
B. Store user profiles
C. Manage DNS
D. Scale VMs

Answer: B. Store user profiles
Reasoning:
User profile disks were used in earlier virtual desktop solutions to store user data separately from the VM. In Azure Virtual Desktop, this concept has largely been replaced by FSLogix profile containers, which provide better performance and flexibility. Profile disks ensure that user data persists across sessions, even when connecting to different hosts. While this concept is still relevant for understanding evolution, FSLogix is now the preferred solution. Profile storage is critical for maintaining user experience in virtual environments.

Q90. What is the role of Azure Advisor in AVD?

A. Store data
B. Provide optimization recommendations
C. Manage DNS
D. Monitor sessions

Answer: B. Provide optimization recommendations
Reasoning:
Azure Advisor analyzes Azure resources and provides recommendations for improving performance, security, reliability, and cost efficiency. In Azure Virtual Desktop, it can suggest actions such as resizing VMs, enabling backups, or improving security configurations. These insights help administrators optimize their environment without manual analysis. Azure Advisor does not store data, manage DNS, or directly

monitor sessions, but it complements monitoring tools by offering actionable guidance. It is a valuable tool for maintaining an efficient and well-optimized AVD deployment.

Q91. What is the purpose of host pool type selection in AVD design?

A. Manage DNS
B. Define user-to-VM assignment model
C. Store data
D. Monitor performance

Answer: B. Define user-to-VM assignment model
Reasoning:
Choosing the host pool type—pooled or personal—is a critical design decision in Azure Virtual Desktop. It determines how users are assigned to virtual machines. In pooled host pools, multiple users share session hosts, making it cost-efficient and scalable. In personal host pools, each user gets a dedicated VM, offering persistence and customization. This decision impacts cost, performance, and user experience. It does not directly manage DNS, store data, or monitor performance, but it defines the overall architecture of the AVD deployment. Selecting the appropriate host pool type ensures that the environment aligns with user requirements and organizational goals.

Q92. Which feature helps maintain consistent application availability in AVD?

A. Azure DNS
B. Application groups
C. Azure Backup
D. Azure Policy

Answer: B. Application groups
Reasoning:
Application groups in Azure Virtual Desktop ensure that users consistently receive access to assigned desktops or applications. By grouping resources logically and assigning them to users, administrators can control what users see and access. This ensures consistency across sessions and simplifies management. If an application is updated or changed, it can be managed centrally within the group. Azure DNS handles name resolution, Backup protects data, and Policy enforces rules. Application groups are essential for delivering a reliable and consistent user experience in AVD.

Q93. What is the purpose of session host health checks?

A. Store profiles
B. Ensure VM readiness and availability
C. Manage DNS
D. Scale VMs

Answer: B. Ensure VM readiness and availability
Reasoning:
Session host health checks verify that virtual machines are ready to accept user connections. They monitor factors such as agent status, connectivity, and system performance. If a host fails a health check, it can be removed from the pool temporarily to prevent users from connecting to a faulty machine. This

improves reliability and user experience by ensuring only healthy hosts are used. Health checks do not store profiles or manage DNS, but they are critical for maintaining system stability and preventing disruptions.

Q94. Which feature is used to control user environment settings in AVD?

A. Group Policy
B. Azure Backup
C. Azure DNS
D. Azure Monitor

Answer: A. Group Policy
Reasoning:
Group Policy is used to configure and manage user and computer settings in Azure Virtual Desktop environments. It allows administrators to enforce policies such as security settings, desktop configurations, and application restrictions. Group Policy can be applied through Active Directory or Azure AD Domain Services. It ensures consistency and compliance across all session hosts. Backup, DNS, and Monitor do not control user environments. Group Policy is a powerful tool for managing user experience and maintaining organizational standards.

Q95. What is the purpose of FSLogix Cloud Cache?

A. Backup only
B. Provide profile redundancy across multiple locations
C. Manage DNS
D. Scale VMs

Answer: B. Provide profile redundancy across multiple locations
Reasoning:
FSLogix Cloud Cache allows profile containers to be stored in multiple locations simultaneously, providing redundancy and high availability. If one storage location becomes unavailable, the system can continue using another copy without disrupting user sessions. This improves resilience and ensures uninterrupted access to user profiles. It is particularly useful in disaster recovery scenarios. Cloud Cache does not manage DNS or scale VMs, but it enhances reliability and fault tolerance in AVD environments.

Q96. Which feature helps reduce storage usage of user profiles?

A. Increase VM size
B. FSLogix exclusions
C. Azure DNS
D. Azure Policy

Answer: B. FSLogix exclusions
Reasoning:
FSLogix exclusions allow administrators to exclude unnecessary files and folders from user profiles, reducing storage usage and improving performance. By using the redirections.xml file, temporary files and caches can be excluded, resulting in smaller profile sizes and faster login times. This optimization is important in large environments where storage costs can be significant. Increasing VM size or using DNS

and Policy does not reduce profile storage. Proper profile management is key to maintaining efficiency and performance in AVD.

Q97. What is the role of Azure Load Balancer in AVD?

A. Manage DNS
B. Distribute traffic across backend resources
C. Store data
D. Monitor sessions

Answer: B. Distribute traffic across backend resources
Reasoning:
Azure Load Balancer distributes incoming network traffic across multiple backend resources, ensuring high availability and reliability. In AVD, it can be used in supporting infrastructure scenarios to balance traffic efficiently. It helps prevent overload on individual components and improves system resilience. Load balancing within AVD host pools is handled separately, but Azure Load Balancer can complement network-level distribution. It does not manage DNS, store data, or monitor sessions directly. It is a key networking component for scalable architectures.

Q98. What is the purpose of Azure Monitor Workbooks in AVD?

A. Store data
B. Visualize and analyze monitoring data
C. Manage DNS
D. Scale VMs

Answer: B. Visualize and analyze monitoring data
Reasoning:
Azure Monitor Workbooks provide interactive dashboards that visualize and analyze data collected from Azure Virtual Desktop. They allow administrators to explore metrics such as session performance, connection health, and resource utilization. Workbooks help identify trends, troubleshoot issues, and optimize the environment. They do not store data or manage DNS, but they provide valuable insights for decision-making. Workbooks are an essential tool for monitoring and maintaining AVD environments.

Q99. Which feature ensures secure communication between AVD components?

A. FTP
B. HTTPS and encryption
C. Telnet
D. Public IP

Answer: B. HTTPS and encryption
Reasoning:
Azure Virtual Desktop uses secure communication protocols such as HTTPS and encryption to protect data in transit. This ensures that user sessions, credentials, and application data are transmitted securely between the client and session host. Encryption prevents unauthorized access and protects sensitive information. FTP and Telnet are insecure protocols and are not used in AVD. Public IP exposure increases

risk. Secure communication is a fundamental requirement for cloud environments, making encryption a critical feature in AVD.

Q100. What is the ultimate goal of Azure Virtual Desktop design?

A. Increase VM count
B. Deliver secure, scalable, and cost-effective virtual desktops
C. Manage DNS
D. Store data

Answer: B. Deliver secure, scalable, and cost-effective virtual desktops
Reasoning:
The ultimate goal of Azure Virtual Desktop design is to provide users with a secure, scalable, and cost-effective virtual desktop experience. This involves balancing performance, security, and cost while ensuring reliability and ease of management. A well-designed AVD environment should meet user needs, protect data, and optimize resource usage. Increasing VM count alone does not achieve this goal and may increase costs unnecessarily. DNS and storage are supporting components but not the primary objective. The focus should always be on delivering a high-quality user experience while maintaining efficiency and security.